GIBBON
and his world

GIBBON
and his world

BY SIR GAVIN DE BEER

A STUDIO BOOK

THE VIKING PRESS · NEW YORK

Published in 1968 by the Viking Press, Inc., 625 Madison Avenue, New York, N.Y. 10022

Printed in Great Britain by Jarrold and Sons Ltd Norwich

PREFACE

It might be thought that since Gibbon left such masterly *Memoirs*, now available in Georges Bonnard's definitive critical edition, D. M. Low wrote an excellent standard *Life*, and J. W. Swain a penetrating analysis of Gibbon's thoughts, a new biography would be an impertinence. Yet Gibbon did not say everything, and I have to offer some fruits of research, matured for nearly twenty years.

The genealogy of the leading families of Lausanne has revealed the head of the chain of causes which resulted in Gibbon's being sent there, the most important event in his life. His earliest extant manuscript, describing a tour of Switzerland when he was a boy, has been edited and published and shows how his future career was then already predictable. A scrap of paper, kindly lent by Sir Geoffrey Keynes, contained a theory of aesthetics which explains Gibbon's appreciation of mountain scenery. References to Gibbon by visitors of different nationalities fill in the picture of his manner of living, and by pointing out his foibles make him more lifelike, if personally less attractive. The medical details of his illness, the correspondence exchanged between his surgeons and Sir Joseph Banks, and a manuscript in the Archives of the Royal Society, reveal the cause of his death.

If the reader reaches far enough, he will receive two shocks to whatever opinion he may have held regarding Gibbon. One comes from a letter (found in the Archives at Lausanne by Professor Jean-Charles Biaudet), the writer of which I identified, the other from a passage in Lady Holland's journal which the late Lord Ilchester kindly communicated to me. I hesitated long before deciding to reveal their contents, but resolved to do so because they are part of the man, and I hope that these trifles may instil a feeling of sympathy for Gibbon in the infirmity from which he suffered, and perhaps even increase admiration for his works.

I should like to take this opportunity of expressing my thanks to Monsieur Jacques Bonnard, Curator of the Musée du Vieux Lausanne, for his help in this field which his father had made so much his own.

GAVIN DE BEER

Gibbon's father, Edward Gibbon

Map of Putney. The Gibbons' house was just
below the T of 'PUTNEY' on the map

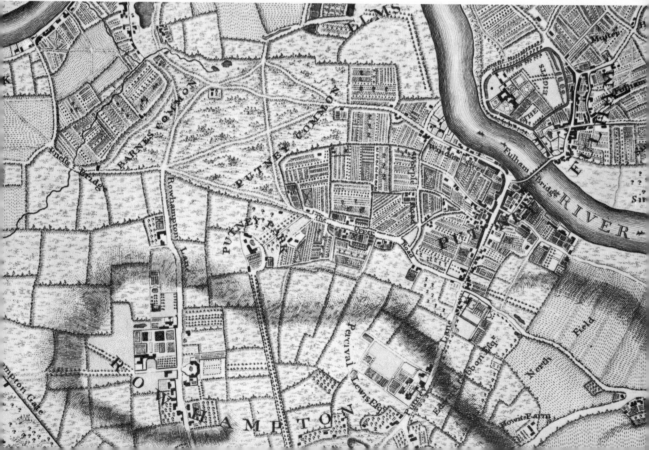

Lime Grove, Gibbon's birthplace, as it was in 1800

WHEN A FATHER has successive sons baptized with the same Christian name, to preserve it in the family, it argues a poor expectation of life for the eldest, and this was the case with Edward Gibbon who was born on 27 April Old Style 1737, 8 May New Style, in a house at the corner of Upper Richmond Road and Putney Park Lane, in Putney. The house was subsequently known as Lime Grove.

His father, also Edward Gibbon, was a colourless country gentleman, twice Member of Parliament, living on what was left of the fortune of grandfather Edward Gibbon, army contractor, Commissioner of Customs, and a Director of the South Sea Company. After the pricking of the South Sea Bubble, Parliament's Bill of Pains and Penalties mulcted him of £96,000 out of £106,000. There was a good deal left, however, in real property, including the estate at Putney and the manors of Buriton and Maple Durham in Hampshire and Lenborough in Buckinghamshire, and the old man then set about making more money.

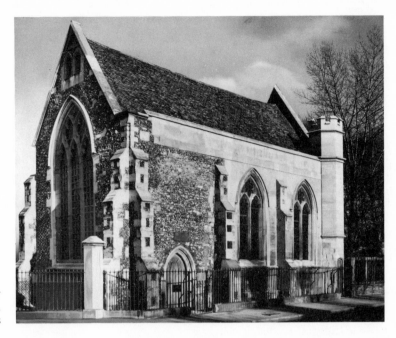

The Porten family, a portrait by William Hogarth

Kingston Grammar School Chapel, in Kingston-on-Thames

Gibbon's mother was Judith Porten, who bore five more sons and one daughter, all of whom died within one year, so that only the weakly first-born lived to bear the name of Edward. But it was touch-and-go with him; he was 'nearly starved by a nurse that had lost her milk', bitten by a dog suspected of rabies, and inoculated with surprising success for smallpox. 'From Sir Hans Sloane and Dr Mead to Ward and the chevalier Taylor every practitioner, both regular and empiric, was alternately summoned; the fees of Doctors were swelled by the bills of Apothecaries and Surgeons; there was a time when I swallowed almost as much Physic as food; and my body is still marked with the scars of bleeding, issues, and caustics.'

The care of the boy devolved largely on his aunt, Catherine Porten, who looked after the sickly, puny child, nursed him through his illnesses, and imparted to him the first rudiments of knowledge. Posterity owes her a debt as chiefly responsible for rearing him. His education began at home and at a day-school in Putney, and when he was seven he was placed in the hands of a tutor, the Rev. John Kirkby, who taught him the elements of arithmetic and Latin; but this period came to an abrupt end when the poor man forgot to include the name of the King in the prayers which he read in the parish church, a dangerous omission so soon after the '45 Rebellion, and was dismissed.

Next, Gibbon was sent to a school in Kingston-on-Thames under Dr Richard Wooddesdon, who had been Chaplain at Magdalen College, Oxford, and counted among his other pupils William Hayley, an institution and a man with whom Gibbon was later to become connected. In December 1746, when he was nine years old, Gibbon's mother died and he was removed from Kingston School. For most of 1747 he lived in a house near Putney Bridge belonging to his grandfather, James Porten, who then promptly went bankrupt. As the house and its contents were not sold immediately, Gibbon was able to enjoy its library which opened his mind to the world of learning.

In January 1748 he was sent to Westminster School, and here again his guardian angel of an aunt, Catherine Porten, came to the rescue, for she opened a boarding-house for Westminster boys in Great College Street, and Gibbon was shielded there from the full force of the tempest of a public school, 'a cavern of fear and sorrow', in which he climbed painfully into the Third Form, with the help of elementary Latin, but no Greek.

Ill-health stepped in again to interrupt the even flow of his studies, and in the summer of 1750 Catherine Porten took him to Bath where he was left under the care of a maidservant. From there he was removed after a few months and taken to Winchester, where Dr Langrish, a physician, endeavoured to cure him; but on his failure Gibbon was again removed to Bath, to benefit from its waters. During this stay in the West Country, he also went on a visit with his

A contemporary painting of Westminster School Hall, London

Great College Street, Westminster, where Gibbon's aunt kept a
boarding-house for Westminster students

father to Mr Hoare's house at Stourhead in Wiltshire, where he became fas-
cinated by a book that he found in the sumptuous library. It was the continuation of Laurence Eachard's *History of the Latin Roman Empire*. 'I was
immersed in the passage of the Goths over the Danube, when the summons of
the dinner-bell reluctantly dragged me from my intellectual feast.'

This feast may have done him more good than physicians or waters, for
gradually his health improved: 'my constitution was fortified and fixed: and
my disorders, instead of growing with my growth and strengthening with my
strength, most wonderfully vanished'. Hopes were revived of his successful
education, and the much-disturbed boy was sent to the Rev. Philip Francis at
Esher, 'in a pleasant spot which promised to unite the various benefits of air,
exercise, and study'. Unfortunately, 'the tutor's spirit was too lively for his
profession: and while he indulged himself in the pleasures of London, his
pupils were left idle at Esher in the custody of a Dutch Usher, of low manners
and contemptible learning'.

After this fresh false start, at his wit's end to know what to do with his son, Gibbon's father sent him to Magdalen College, Oxford.

Magdalen College, Oxford

During his ailing years, the boy had, not unnaturally, taken refuge in reading, but it had been desultory, and he 'arrived at Oxford with a stock of erudition that might have puzzled a Doctor, and a degree of ignorance of which a school-boy would have been ashamed'. A Gentleman-Commoner, fifteen years old, he was admitted to Magdalen College on 3 April 1752, and given well-furnished rooms in the stately block of the New Buildings. He felt suddenly promoted from the servitude of a boy to the freedom of a man, and a man of dignity, for his status entitled him to wear a velvet mortarboard and a silk gown. Instead of being hounded by the sound of the dinner-bell, he came into Hall in his own time, late. He might have stood on the threshold of a productive and useful period of his life, but that was not to be, because security and sloth, not industriousness and endeavour, were the characteristics of his professors and tutors, and senior members of the University were copied by their juniors.

Magdalen College, Oxford; an early eighteenth-century view

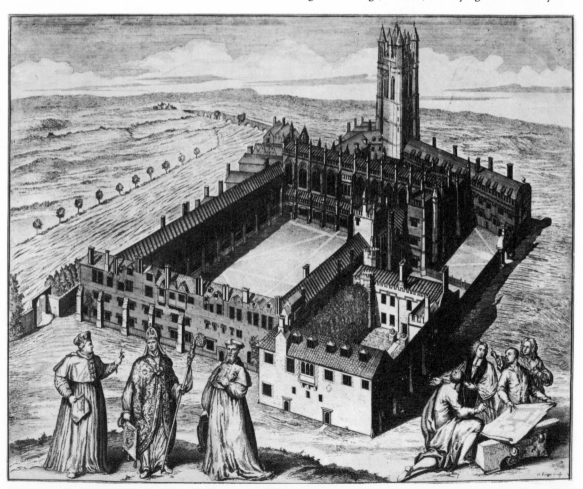

A Gentleman Commoner of the
University of Oxford, 1792

His first tutor was Dr Thomas Waldegrave, with whom he began reading
daily the comedies of Terence and other Latin plays. After a few weeks,
Gibbon found his tutorials so dull that he tried playing truant, and was com-
placently excused by his tutor. No essays were required of him, and no plan of
study was prescribed for him, so the employment of his mind and time was
left to his own devices. Deficient as he was in basic learning and in logical
thinking, he had already acquired a sufficient taste for exotic history to lead him
to compose an essay, 'The Age of Sesostris', in which he tried his hand at
emendations of the calendar to determine the date of his reign. After all, his
own calendar had just been emended, when eleven days were struck off the
long vacation in September 1752, by the adoption of the Gregorian Style in
Great Britain.

Dr Waldegrave retired to a country living, and Gibbon 'was transferred with
the rest of his livestock to a senior Fellow', Dr Thomas Winchester, of whom
Gibbon had to say that he 'well remembered that he had a salary to receive,
and only forgot that he had a duty to perform'. Gibbon was never summoned to
a single lecture or tutorial, and paid only one, voluntary visit to his tutor's

Magdalen College New Buildings, in a drawing of 1787

rooms. It was not surprising that, in this atmosphere of complete indifference to his moral and academic welfare, Gibbon's attention and inclinations strayed into different fields. He absented himself repeatedly, and visited Bath, Buckinghamshire and went four times to London without any check by the College authorities on his behaviour.

Undergraduates were required to subscribe to the Oath of Supremacy, but as Gibbon was so young when he matriculated he was told to subscribe when he was sixteen. He omitted to present himself, however, and the Vice-Chancellor forgot to summon him. When he came to write his *Memoirs*, nearly forty years later, Gibbon's memory tricked him into confusing the Oath of Supremacy with the Thirty-Nine Articles of Faith of the Church of England, which he did sign.

Gibbon as a young man

Conyers Middleton had recently published his revolutionary book, *A Free Enquiry. . .* , in which he concluded that there was no reason to believe that miraculous powers continued in the Church after the days of the Apostles. The effect of this contention on Gibbon was to drive him in precisely the opposite direction, and to lead him to become more and more impressed with the merits of celibacy, monastic life, the cross, holy oil, images, invocation of saints, worship of relics, belief in Purgatory, and the mystery of transubstantiation. On visits to London, he felt too bashful to accompany his friends to the taverns and brothels of Covent Garden, but there was one visit he did make which was important because it embarked him on a course of thought and action that was, again, to interrupt the chequered career that went by the name of his education.

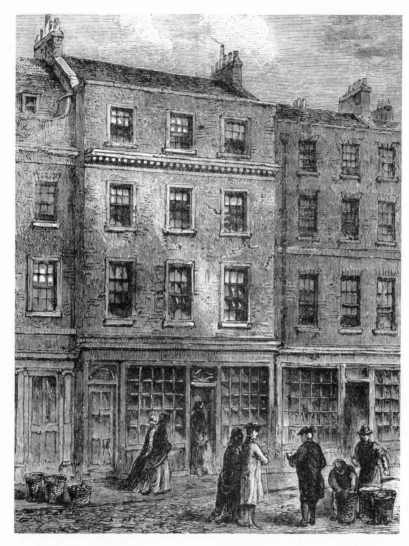

Russell Street,
Covent Garden, London

Conversion   Gibbon was, as he said, by his own convictions already half converted to
to Rome   the Roman faith when he met Mr Molesworth, who had travelled further on
the same path. Through him, Gibbon had an opportunity of reading an
English translation of the works of Bossuet, and his conversion was complete.
Militant Protestant opinion was already alerted to the danger of this very thing
happening to Oxford undergraduates, and Gibbon trod warily. On one of
his visits to London he called on John Lewis, a Roman Catholic bookseller
in Russell Street, Covent Garden (dangerous neighbourhood), and by him
was recommended to a Jesuit priest, Father Bernard Baker, Chaplain to the

Sardinian Ambassador, in whose chapel in Lincoln's Inn Fields, on 8 June 1753, Gibbon was received into the Roman Catholic Church.

He wrote to his father to inform him and to glory in the step which he had just taken; but his father, deeply shocked and angered, threatening banishment and disinheritance, unfortunately broached the matter, and once the secret was out, the consequences had to be faced.

Gibbon afterwards admitted that he was not sufficiently informed of the dangers which he ran. Contemporary records contain more than one instance of Bills of Indictment found against priests who had made converts to Rome, which amounted to committing high treason. According to Lord Sheffield, John Lewis was summoned to appear before the Privy Council, with what result is not known; but in Gibbon's own case the result was immediate exclusion from the University of Oxford. So ended his connection with Magdalen College.

Roman Catholic Chapel, Lincoln's Inn Fields, where Gibbon was received into the Roman Catholic Church at the age of 16

Confronted with this new crisis in his son's affairs, Gibbon's father first took the curious step of sending him to David Mallet, something of a free-thinker, who lived in Putney, but it failed to reclaim Gibbon, who was rather scandalized by his new mentor's philosophy. Something more drastic had to be done, and Gibbon was banished to Lausanne, partly as a punishment, and partly as an expiation and cure for his theological distemper.

It would not occur to any young Englishman today to consider that a stay in Lausanne was either a banishment or a punishment, and it is not uninteresting to inquire why it should have been so in Gibbon's case. There were three reasons why it would not ordinarily have occurred to an English father in the middle of the eighteenth century to send his son to Lausanne. The first was that Geneva was the usual choice; it had long supplied the needs of a French education guaranteed to be free from the perils of popery. The Matriculation Register of the Academy of Geneva is full of illustrious names from the middle of the sixteenth century to the end of the eighteenth. Whether members of the University or not, they all too frequently behaved very badly, like Henry St John, afterwards Viscount Bolingbroke, who was guilty of an affray in the streets when he fought with Isaac Rousseau, father of Jean-Jacques, or Henry William, Lord Paget, afterwards Earl of Uxbridge and Marquess of Anglesey, for whom the Duke of Gloucester interceded with the civic authorities to release him from gaol. But the very fact that young Englishmen were so numerous at Geneva, badly behaved and drawn from such a high and frivolous level of society, would have been a deterrent to Gibbon's father from sending his son there.

Another reason why Lausanne would not have occurred to an English father as a place in which to study French, lay in the fact that after the conquest of the Pays de Vaud (of which Lausanne is the capital) by the Canton of Berne in 1536, Lausanne was governed by, and part of, a German-speaking State. The few early English travellers who passed through it sometimes expressed surprise at finding that the language spoken at Lausanne was French.

Finally, it was not so very long since the inhabitants of the Pays de Vaud, and especially those of Lausanne and Vevey, had granted asylum and protection to the regicides, Edmund Ludlow, Andrew Broughton, John Phelps and many others. This harbouring of the King's enemies was further compounded when the conspirators of the Rye House Plot – Richard Nelthorpe, John Rowe and Nathaniel Wade – were similarly granted asylum. A patriotic Englishman, particularly one for whom the House of Stuart still had attractions as in Gibbon's family, might have recoiled from sending his son among such radicals as the inhabitants of Lausanne.

A French diligence of the eighteenth century

This tacit ban was broken and a new fashion set by the Earl of Chesterfield, who wanted his bastard son, Philip Stanhope (to whom the famous *Letters* were addressed), to have a widened education. Lord Chesterfield had a secretary, Solomon Dayrolles, whose two cousins Madeleine and Suzanne Françoise de Teissonnière d'Ayrolles, married respectively Charles Guillaume de Loys de Bochat and Samuel Deyverdun, and belonged to the highest society in Lausanne. It was clearly because of Dayrolles's family connections that young Stanhope was sent there in 1746, with his tutor Walter Harte and a youthful companion, Edward Eliot. Eliot, who was shortly to marry Gibbon's first cousin, Katherine Elliston, and was afterwards to become Lord Eliot and to play an important part in Gibbon's life, originated the idea when, from his own experience, he advised Mr Gibbon to send Edward there. Accordingly, under the care of a Swiss, Henry Frey, Gibbon was packed off on 19 June 1753, taken from Dover to Calais, and through Saint Quentin, Rheims, Langres and Besançon to Lausanne, where he arrived on 30 June.

At Lausanne   At Lausanne Gibbon was placed under the care of the Rev. Daniel Pavillard, who is generally referred to as a Calvinist minister, and was indeed so described by Gibbon himself. It is true that when the Reformation was introduced into the Pays de Vaud by the victorious armies and pastors of Berne, the theology of that French-speaking province was close to that of the famous reformer of Geneva. But by the middle of the eighteenth century, a change had set in. The government of Berne, which never allowed the Church to gain the ascendancy which it enjoyed in Geneva, kept a close control even on the theology of its pastors, and the more easy-going way of life practised by the prosperous Canton

A contemporary view of Lausanne, where Gibbon arrived in 1753

of Berne, influenced by the milder Zwinglian creed of Zürich, led to a relaxation of the austerity of Calvinist tenets, particularly as regards predestination and grace, with the result that the theology preached at Lausanne was more liberal. This was not without its importance in the success of Pavillard's persuasion of Gibbon to return to the Reformed faith.

On his arrival at Lausanne, almost everything might have been calculated to harden his opposition to his treatment. His ignorance of French at first made even conversation impossible, and he felt isolated, all the more because he was disappointed in his expectation that Roman Catholic contacts would find and

The Reverend Daniel Pavillard,
Gibbon's mentor in Lausanne

encourage him in his exile. Instead of living in comfortable and dignified surroundings, with adequate money, he now found himself confined to a very modest lodging (16 Rue Cité-Derrière, since pulled down), an earthenware stove instead of the comfort of an open fire, a pittance of pocket-money, no servant, inconvenient set hours for meals the quantity, quality and cooking of which he found sadly unsatisfying, while the dirty table-cloth and the un-sympathetic appearance and manners of Mme Pavillard served to reinforce the painful realization that he had been degraded. It speaks highly of Pavillard's wise and sympathetic handling of his pupil that his reconversion was successful, and that, from the first impression of being confined in a prison, Gibbon gradually learned to appreciate, and soon to love the town of Lausanne, from which he derived inestimable benefits to his education and his views on life.

The rapidity of his progress in learning French astonished even him, and he soon found himself more at home in that language than in English. Pavillard gradually led him to the study of modern history and geography, French and Latin classics and philosophy. Gibbon devised for himself a rigorous method of exercise, which was to translate a classical Latin text into French, leave it aside until it was no longer fresh in his mind, and then translate it back into

Latin to compare with the original. He divided the Latin classics into historians, poets, orators and philosophers, covered them from Plautus to the decline of the Empire and made notes of them. His knowledge of these impelled him to become familiar with the Greek classics, and he soon knew enough of that language to enjoy Homer, Xenophon and Herodotus, who took their places beside Cicero, Virgil, Terence, Horace, Quintilian, Tacitus and many others. Mathematics, algebra and conic sections were not neglected. He also studied commentaries on John Locke which introduced him to political principles, Pascal's *Provinciales*, the life of Julian the Apostate by the Abbé de la Bletterie, and Giannone's *Civil History of Naples*, all of which stimulated his powers of original thought and judgment, and contributed towards the line of work which he was eventually to follow.

Questions of religion were approached by Pavillard in an indirect and skilful manner. He left certain books about, correctly suspecting that Gibbon would take them away and read them. Step by step, the tenets of Roman doctrine were discussed and disposed of, 'after a firm and well-managed defence'. Lord Sheffield afterwards recalled the astonishment with which Pavillard 'gazed on Gibbon standing before him, a thin little figure, with a large head, disputing and urging, with the greatest ability, all the best arguments that had ever been used in favour of popery'.

Pavillard's house in Lausanne, where Gibbon lodged during his first stay in that city

M. de Polier de Bottens
and his wife

Just as his conversion to Rome had been primarily the result of his own reflections, so his return to Protestantism was ultimately his own persuasion. With a candour and simplicity that are baffling, he recalled his satisfaction on realizing that whereas only one sense, sight used for reading, supports the doctrine of transubstantiation, three senses, sight, touch and taste, contradict it. It is not clear whether this conclusion was due to his ignorance of the Catholic doctrine which denies that the substance is accessible to the senses, or to a victory of rationalism over theological subtlety.

Eighteen months after Gibbon's arrival in Lausanne, his tutor judged that he had learned his Catechism, and after Antoine-Noé de Polier de Bottens, First Pastor of Lausanne, had examined him, he was admitted to communion on Christmas Day 1754. The main object in sending him to Lausanne had been achieved, but his wish to return home was firmly repulsed by his father, and he had to wait a further four years. Posterity can only be glad of it.

Tour of Switzerland

In 1755, Gibbon obtained his father's approval for him to make a tour of Switzerland. Pavillard, his wife and Gibbon set off from Lausanne on 21 September, on what turned out to be a practical course of instruction in the history, geography, politics and constitutions of the more important Cantons of Switzerland. 'We travelled slowly in a coach through the principal towns,

Grofs Baden

Limat fluu

Berne, one of the stops on Gibbon's Swiss tour

The city of Zürich

The Abbey of Einsiedeln, in Canton Schwyz

Neuchâtel, Bienne, Soleure, Aarau, Baden, Zürich, Basle, and Berne, and visited in every place the persons and things best worthy of our attention.' Then follows a passage which testifies to Pavillard's success: 'At the rich Abbey of Einsiedeln, the Swiss Loretto, I viewed with the contempt of a protestant and a philosopher the Idolatrous worship of our Lady of the Hermits.'

Gibbon wrote a journal of his Swiss tour which, although the oldest extant manuscript from his pen, has only recently been published. In it he shows that he is already well versed in ancient history, and particularly that of Rome. He makes appropriate quotations from Sallust and compares the Roman Republic with that of Berne. At Baden, a special commission was sitting to sort out the political troubles of the Valley of Toggenburg, and Gibbon was introduced to the Bernese delegates, Johann-Anton Tillier and Beat-Siegmund Ougs-burger, elder statesmen of the highest offices, who were so kind as to receive the eighteen-year-old youth, and to explain the political problem to him.

The trouble was that the sovereign of Toggenburg, the Abbot of Saint-Gall, was constantly at loggerheads with the inhabitants of Toggenburg, who were Protestant. They complained, in addition, that they were liable for military service in regiments raised by the abbot for the benefit of any nation that he ordered. They insisted that they should conduct their own foreign policy, make alliances with whom they chose and raise regiments themselves if they wished to do so. This was the political nut that the commission had to crack, and an object lesson for Gibbon.

In the library at Zürich he saw the Carolingian manuscript Bible, in which mention of the 'three Heavenly witnesses' (1 John v. 8) is missing; and in the library of the Abbey of Saint-Urban he showed that he was already familiar with the importance of collected texts as sources for the study of history, and enumerated those of Graevius, Gronovius, Montfaucon, Muratori and the Byzantine writers.

At Berne, Gibbon met one of the greatest men of the century, Albrecht von Haller, poet, physiologist, botanist and philosopher, who talked to him about the books which he was then writing. As von Haller had at least six books on the stocks at that time, Gibbon must have enjoyed the opportunity of seeing books at many stages of production. He also met a young man of his own age, Friedrich Schmidt, who had already made important archaeological discoveries of Roman remains at Avenches, the old capital of the Helvetii.

The Charnel House at Morat

Albrecht von Haller,
the scholar whom
Gibbon met at Berne

During the tour, Gibbon passed three battlefields, those of Grandson and Morat where Charles the Bold of Burgundy was routed, and Fraubrunnen where a monument had been erected to commemorate a victory of the Swiss over the English in 1375, with a Latin inscription in which he found two gross historical mistakes. A point of interest arises here from the fact that his commonplace-book shows that Gibbon had read about the Fraubrunnen inscription in March 1755; he had therefore prepared for his journey which, from all points of view, was an unqualified success. It was finished on 20 October, and as it cost only thirty-five louis, the money was well spent. It will also be noticed that some of the roads in his mind already led to the Roman Empire.

There had been some other Englishmen at Lausanne, including a West‑minster School friend, Lord Huntingtower, but as Gibbon's position and means made him unable to associate with them on equal terms, he avoided them, though not before he had got himself into a scrape with a plausible ne'er‑do‑well, Mr Gee, to whom he lost 110 guineas playing faro. Gee also sold him a watch and a horse, the debt to be repaid in England. Out of his mind with worry at the follies he had committed, Gibbon escaped on the horse to Geneva where he tried to sell it, and where Pavillard found him and brought him back. The debt was subsequently reduced to fifty guineas, and the experience was cheaply bought at the price.

Cut off from English society, Gibbon more than compensated himself by cultivating that of the inhabitants of Lausanne. He was soon received in the homes of the best families, and in this manner formed an intimate life‑long friendship with Georges Deyverdun, son of that Mme Deyverdun, cousin of Solomon Dayrolles who, through Lord Chesterfield and Edward Eliot, was at the head of the chain of circumstances that led to Gibbon's being sent to Lausanne. Deyverdun's mother had died and he was living with his aunt, Mme de Bochat, the other cousin of Dayrolles.

The lion of society during Gibbon's stay at Lausanne was Voltaire, and it is a further tribute to the liberality of the clergy of that town that the man who invited the old unbeliever to come was Polier de Bottens, Gibbon's catechizer. Voltaire first took a house called Monrion, and afterwards another called Mon Repos, where he indulged in his favourite pastime of putting on and acting himself in plays of his own authorship. 'He received me with civility as an English youth', and, had Gibbon known it, a later friend of his, Oliver Goldsmith, also made Voltaire's acquaintance at that time.

At Mon Repos, Gibbon saw performances of *Zaïre*, *Alzire*, *Zulime*, *L'Enfant prodigue* and *Fanime*, with Voltaire playing the parts of Lusignan, Alvarez, Benassar, Euphemon and Mohadar, names not without interest for the sequel. 'My ardour, which soon became conspicuous, seldom failed of procuring me a ticket; . . . and, however addicted to study, I enjoyed my share of the amusements of Society. After the representations at Mon Repos I some‑times supped with the Actors.' These were 'a troop of Gentlemen and Ladies', as befitted amateur theatricals, and this chance of meeting them widened still further Gibbon's circle of friends.

With the growth of his self‑assurance, the progress of Gibbon's studies carried him on the crest of a wave. While reading Livy, he was struck by a word that did not make sense in the speech by Hannibal after the surrender of Carthage (Book xxx, Chapter 44), so he wrote to Jean‑Baptiste Crevier in Paris, who had published an edition of Livy, to suggest an emendation of one

Voltaire, who was
living in Lausanne
at the time Gibbon was
being educated there

letter – by substituting the word *otio* ('inactivity') for *odio* ('hatred'), a suggestion gladly accepted by the master. The emendation agrees with the text of the oldest extant manuscript reading of this passage, in Codex Colbertinus, and the whole passage reads *nec est cur vos otio vestro consultum ab romanis credatis* ('you must not think that it is for your tranquillity that the Romans have regard'). It is the reading accepted today.

Johann Jacob Breitinger,
Librarian of Zürich,
with whom Gibbon, aged 19,
maintained a correspondence in Latin

Having acquired the habit and taste of communicating with leading scholars of the day, Gibbon started a correspondence in Latin with Johann Jacob Breitinger, the Librarian of Zürich, on questions of ancient history and classical texts, and although the replies he received were censorious, he felt encouraged by the knowledge that he was at any rate able to debate with such a scholar. Another correspondence with François-Louis Allamand, Pastor of Bex, 'a master of language of science, and above all of dispute', on the subject of Locke's metaphysics, enabled Gibbon 'by fencing with so skillful a master', to acquire 'some dexterity in the use of my philosophical weapons'.

It was not long before Gibbon tried his hand at making use of these weapons, his knowledge and his already considerable little stock of experience, and he started writing an *Essai sur l'étude de la littérature*. It was prompted by his reaction against the policy of the French *philosophes*, such as d'Alembert, to denigrate scholars and students of classical literature and ancient history under the contemptuous title of *érudits*, and to extol 'philosophers' who painted with a very broad brush and ever broader imagination. Gibbon was so deeply attached to his classical authors and the details of ancient history, that he provided the incongruous spectacle of a young Englishman flying to the defence of the French Académie des Inscriptions, then held in low esteem in its own country. Gibbon took this work up again and completed it after his return to England.

Gibbon's journal for June 1757 contains the entry: 'Saw Mademoiselle Curchod. *Omnia vincit amor et nos cedamus amori*', from which the reader should not jump to premature conclusions, but learn that Gibbon had naïvely and chastely fallen head over heels in love. Suzanne Curchod was the daughter of the Pastor of the small village of Crassier, on the slopes of the Jura between Lausanne and Geneva. Her family was of slender means, but she combined charm with virtue and learning with grace; 'in her short visits to some relations at Lausanne, the wit and beauty and erudition of Mademoiselle Curchod were the theme of universal applause'. She was the moving spirit among a group of young people who constituted the 'Société du Printemps', which frequently met in the country – then completely rural just outside the town – where they picnicked and played innocent games, giving each other fanciful mythological names. The extent of Gibbon's infatuation for the girl, who was known to everybody as 'la belle Curchod', may be gauged from a story, however apocryphal, that circulated about him, to the effect that he roamed the fields, a drawn dagger in his hand, summoning all and sundry to agree that Mlle Curchod was the most beautiful woman in the world.

In love: Suzanne Curchod

Crassier, the village where Suzanne Curchod lived

There is a description of Gibbon by Suzanne: she will pass lightly over his appearance; he has pretty hair, dainty hands and the bearing of a person of quality. His countenance is so lively and remarkable that she has never seen anybody like him. His face has so much expression that there is nearly always something new to be seen in it. His gestures are so appropriate that they reinforce the words he speaks. In a word, his person is so out of the ordinary that one is never tired of looking at him, painting him and copying him. He knows the respect that is due to women, and his manners are easy without familiarity. He is not a good dancer. In short, he has but few of the characteristics that distinguish a coxcomb. His wit ranges over a vast territory.

It will be noticed that she does not say that he is handsome or well built: he was less than five feet tall with a big head, bulging forehead, round eyes and a small squat nose between chubby cheeks. But she emphasizes that his qualities are intellectual and this his mind is original.

So began a love story that never became an 'affair', the details of which are difficult to unravel because they were so wrapped in conventional courtesies. It is clear that at the outset Gibbon was the ardent wooer, and that before very long, although penniless and uncertain of his future, he proposed marriage. Suzanne was receptive but cautious; she had another suitor, M. de Montplaisir, a local man and rich, possibly preferred by her parents, but of mediocre intellect. She also knew that Gibbon had said nothing about his attachment to her to his father, who might object.

The Pastor of Crassier used from time to time to invite students from Lausanne and Geneva to stay in his parsonage, and this Gibbon was soon allowed and encouraged by the girl's parents to do. Seeing the object of his love in the happy midst of her family must have emphasized the difference between this blissful scene and his own condition, banished from his own family as a leper. Furthermore, he had just learned that his father had married again, and to his suspicion of the woman who had usurped the place of his mother was added the apprehension that, if children were born, his own expectations would be diminished.

Presently, Suzanne allowed Gibbon to write to her, and many letters of this correspondence have been preserved. He also wrote verses to her, the only ones he is known ever to have composed in a modern language. They cannot be called poetry because they are so flat, and it seems that they are a *collage* of lines from Benserade, Boileau and others; but this does not mean that they were any less sincere in expressing his adoration.

In his first letter he counts the hours, minutes and seconds since he parted from her at Crassier, and compares himself with an Oriental prince who has changed his throne for a dungeon, and with Adam in *Paradise Lost*. He was

Suzanne Curchod

at her feet, speaking to her of love, and she did not repulse him; but she has now disappointed him by not allowing him to see her at Rolle, whither he was shortly going. Suzanne's reply was couched in terms of similar allegory, but with a little banter. Suppose that Gibbon was Satan or Astaroth, and she Ariel or Gabriel, he must see that if the angel frequented the demon too often, it would be suspect. In fact, she did see him at Rolle.

Gibbon's next letter explains how he has been passing his time, without enjoyment since he last saw her, and that his only consolation is the remembrance of the exquisite moments that he has passed in the company of the most charming of women. He is building castles in the air for the future which he would not exchange for the concrete plans of anybody. He writes again to say that he has emerged from a miserable past since he has known her, and he signs himself 'The Son of King Moabdar' [sic], from which it can be concluded that the fanciful names of the members of the Société du Printemps now included one for Gibbon, and that both Suzanne and he saw Voltaire play Mohadar. Her reply is signed 'Zimerline'. The lovers are indulging in nonsense-talk.

They have a little tiff; he has not told her that he is going to Berne for a few days. Suzanne is now afraid of losing her Englishman and, instead of banter, she says that she suspects him of being unfaithful. Gibbon hastens to protest: 'how could you doubt for one instant my love and my troth?' But he goes on to say that his father has now allowed him to return to England in a letter so tender and full of plans for his future, that he sees in the way of his happiness a mountain of obstacles quite different from the pecuniary difficulties which had been his sole worry. His happiest lot would be to see the time come when he could tell her repeatedly how much he loves her and to hear her say that the object of his love is not ungrateful.

In another letter, as a token of devotion to his living muse, he proposes to dedicate his *Essai* to her. He goes once more to Crassier, where it seems that she accepts his proposal of marriage, but does not want to be distantly separated from her parents. Suzanne's last letter before Gibbon left Lausanne tells him sadly that he must not act against the wishes of his father, or abandon him at his great age (he was, in fact, only fifty) and marry a foreigner whose superiority as a woman perhaps does not exist outside his heart.

It is clear that each was attached to the other, but how deeply in each case, and how painful eventual disappointment would be, it is difficult to be sure.

Return to England   Gibbon's father had given permission for him to return to England, but meanwhile the Seven Years War had broken out, and no Englishman could travel through France without a special passport which, as Voltaire's correspondence with the French Minister, the Duc de Choiseul, showed, was very difficult to obtain. The route through Germany was longer and not devoid of danger because that country was one of the theatres of war. Gibbon decided to pass through France wearing the uniform of an officer in a Swiss regiment in the Dutch service, posing as Georges Deyverdun whose passport he carried, in company with two of his Swiss friends, captains in the regiment. The risk of detection was small because of the excellence of his French, and, as events showed, he got through safely.

Place Stanislas in Nancy, visited by Gibbon on his trip back to England in 1758

Maestricht, another stop during this journey

The Hague, as it appeared about the time Gibbon passed through *en route* to Rotterdam

They left Lausanne on 11 April 1758 and trod French soil at Jougne where, with a number of friends who had accompanied them thus far, they drank perhaps too much in their farewells. Through Ornans, Besançon, Luxeuil and Epinal, they reached Nancy, where Gibbon admired the Place Stanislas and wrote a letter to Suzanne. After passing Metz they entered the Ardennes and slept at Arlon, Bastogne, Marche and Liège before arriving at Maestricht, where Gibbon visited Louis de Beaufort (author of a poor book on Roman history), parted from his companions, and wrote another letter (lost) to Suzanne. After journeying through Bois-le-Duc, The Hague and Rotterdam, he embarked at Brill on 3 May and landed at Harwich on the following day. On 5 May he reached London and went straight to his aunt Catherine Porten, where he learned that his father was in town. That same evening, at Charles Street, St James's, he saw his father and the new Mrs Gibbon and was immediately reconciled to accepting her into the family. He wrote yet another letter (also lost) to Suzanne.

Gibbon came of age on 8 May 1758, and on 29 June his father settled £300 a year on him, after breaking the entail and raising £10,000 on a mortgage with his consent – which was why his return home had become necessary. Gibbon was now independent, but not affluent. He spent the summer at Buriton, and the winter alone in London, at lodgings in New Bond Street.

Gibbon waited three months before broaching to his father the subject that was on his mind and his heart, and met with a firm refusal. On 24 August 1758, he broke the news to Suzanne as gently as he could. He does not know how to begin but he must. From this start she will have gathered what he is going to say; he must give her up for ever. His father's words were 'marry your foreigner, you are independent; but remember before you do so that you are a son and a citizen'. He hopes that she will be happier than he can ever hope to be. This was the situation which Gibbon described dramatically in his *Memoirs* with the words 'I sighed as a lover: I obeyed as a son'. With his sigh went out his flame; he had acquiesced in the easy way out.

Engagement broken

Suzanne's reply is dated 7 September 1758. She is heartbroken; her attach-ment to him is so pure that she is prepared to abandon home, friends and mother-tongue to follow a man whom she thought incapable of abusing her confidence. If he had proposed to his father that, during the lifetime of her father, he leave her in her own country and came over to visit her every other year, such an arrangement could surely not affect his status as a son and a citizen. Has he left nothing undone that might have removed the difficulties?

On 5 November 1758 Suzanne wrote again. She is surprised at his silence, but she has received a letter from his step-mother saying, kindly, that she has intercepted Suzanne's letter, and that further letters would have the same fate. There has been an insinuation by Suzanne's parents that he connived with his step-mother in this practice so as to avoid replying, but she refuses to believe it. Her own mother would be ready to accompany her to England; but if his father is inflexible, he knows her well enough not to need to tell her that nothing could oblige him to fail in his duty. Nor would she wish to incur her own reproach of herself if he did.

To this letter, which did reach him, Gibbon replied on 23 February 1759. He has had difficulty in refraining from overwhelming his step-mother with reproaches for keeping Suzanne's letters from him for six months. He has had nothing to do with the interceptions and proposes an accommodation address for letters to reach him, although he wonders if prudence would not advise ending this correspondence. He thinks constantly of the only woman who could have made him happy, and his friends tax him with being preoccupied and having something on his mind. He has used every argument with his father, who says that even if Mlle Curchod is everything that she is made out to be,

Buriton House, Hampshire, the Gibbons' country home, as it is today

she is a foreigner, while he is only too prone and partial to foreign customs; he has even lost the mastery over his native tongue. At some moments he thinks that he owes his father nothing more; at others he contemplates awaiting his father's death, but this is not a good attitude. And if his father should survive him, what would her position be?

The romance had come up against a wall more impenetrable than that which separated Pyramus and Thisbe. Gibbon knew it and had already accepted it; Suzanne could not bring herself to do so, and the tone of his letters conveyed the impression that he still loved her. Her disappointment may have become known to her friends in Switzerland, if the following curious little incident is relevant. The most widely read magazine in French-speaking Switzerland was the *Journal helvétique* of which the number for June 1759 (by which date Gibbon's last letter would have been received) published an anonymous article entitled 'Eloge du Rat. A Mademoiselle Curchod'. It contained an allusion to La Fontaine's fable 'Le chat et un vieux rat', in which the Alexander of cats, the Attila of rats, covers himself with flour to deceive the rat who is promptly destroyed. This behaviour is compared with that of Cromwell, who borrowed the white mantle of virtue to masquerade as the honest, innocent man, and suddenly pulled off the mask of hypocrisy. There would be point in dedicating this article to Mlle Curchod if the intention were to cast Gibbon in the part of Cromwell, the perfidious Englishman who has deceived her.

Life continued normally enough at Buriton, but in New Bond Street he found himself a stranger in an unknown city. The ordinary pleasures of life were, of course, within reach of any man who cared little for his health, wealth or company, and he said later, with what truth it is difficult to be sure, that the contagion of example sometimes seduced him from the tavern to the play and to the brothel. But the habits that he had formed in Lausanne led him to look higher. Since his father's retirement to the country, his circle of friends, for what they might have been worth, had forgotten him, and Gibbon had to make new ones for himself. But he spent many evenings by himself in his lodgings with his books, interrupting his studies with sighs for Lausanne.

The young gentleman

A Rowlandson view of Bond Street, London, in 1796

Jonathan Swift

Joseph Addison

During the summers at Buriton, life was easier, for the library contained some good editions of the classics, though meal-times were long and he was obliged both to help to receive visitors and to attend dinner-parties away from home. He survived the tedium of Church services by providing himself with a Greek Bible in his pew, but they set him thinking. Gibbon had now been converted twice, an experience that might be expected to lead to a testing of his faith, which it did. He was no longer scandalized by the aggressive scepticism of the Scottish poet, David Mallet, on whose advice he turned his attention to the works of Swift and Addison, followed by those of Robertson and Hume, all of which provided him with his first serious introduction to the English literary tradition. He was greatly struck by Robertson's style. Hume was the author not only of the *History of England*, but of the *Natural History of Religion* and of the 'Essay on Miracles' in his *Philosophical Essays*. Presently Gibbon turned to the French sceptics, Fontenelle (who had recently died in his hundredth year, in 1757) and Pierre Bayle, and thus he was led to test nothing less than the evidence for Christianity itself. He was now well on the way 'from superstition to scepticism'.

David Hume, the Scottish philosopher whose works Gibbon began to read after his return to
England in 1758

Alton, Hampshire, where Captain Gibbon mobilized his company of the South Hampshire Militia on 2 June 1760

The Militia   The harsh remarks about foreigners in Gibbon's father's last refusal to think better of Suzanne Curchod must be seen as a reflection of the war which was now raging, and which was soon to suck his father and himself into its vortex. The government's actions in 1756 in inviting Hessian and Hanoverian troops to defend Britain infuriated Englishmen, who insisted on the establishment of a Militia, with the result that an Act was passed early in 1759. On 12 June Gibbon and his father received commissions as captain and major in the South Hampshire Militia. Admiral Hawke's great victory of Quiberon Bay in November 1759 had removed all reasonable fear of a French invasion, but nevertheless, on 10 May 1760, the Militia (with a derisory strength of 32,000 men) was embodied, and on 2 June Gibbon mobilized his company at Alton. 'It was too late to retreat: it was too early to repent: the Battalion on the 4th of June was assembled at Winchester.'

There followed two and a half years of troublesome duty, in which Gibbon was taxed particularly hard. They marched about from place to place, from Winchester to Blandford, to Porchester, to Cranbrook, to Dover, back to Winchester, to Devizes, to Salisbury, again to Blandford, and to Southampton. During all this time, Gibbon had not only to learn his duties and train his men, but as the Major and the Lieutenant-Colonel were frequently absent, it often fell to Gibbon to exercise and drill the whole battalion. In addition, as he was by far the best educated and most capable officer in the regiment, all the tiresome paper work came his way. In the first place there was a long-drawn-out feud with the Lord-Lieutenant of the County, the Duke of Bolton, over the right to nominate to commands, which led to endless arrests, reports, courts martial, correspondence with the government in London and other time-consuming duties. On one court martial, he had the interesting experience of meeting John Wilkes, of 'infinite wit and humour, and a great deal of knowledge; but a thorough profligate in principle as in practice'. There were also the duties of guarding French prisoners of war; fevers decimated the ranks, and men caught venereal diseases. There is no mention of the officers in this respect although there were visits to brothels.

Grenadier Cap of the
South Hampshire Militia

Blandford Forum, Dorset

Dover: the Castle and the town in 1762, during Gibbon's military service

Mars and Minerva

There can be no doubt that Gibbon was a conscientious and efficient officer, and on 25 June 1761 he was appointed Captain of the Grenadier Company. Throughout his military service, Gibbon always had books with him. A happy interlude combining Minerva with Mars was the publication of his *Essai sur l'étude de la littérature*, on which he had worked since his return to England. It was a combined result of his own ambition to publish a book in a language other than his own, and his father's pride in a son able to do so, and thereby to further his prospects of obtaining employment in a post, possibly diplomatic. Matthew Maty, Librarian in the newly opened British Museum, was consulted on the text, a dedication in English was penned, not to Suzanne but to Gibbon's father, and on 7 July 1761 it was published. In October, the author, 'somewhat disordered with sweat and dust, in the cap, dress, and accoutrements of a captain of Grenadiers', come straight off duty, presented a copy of his first published work to the Duke of York, in camp. Some dozens of copies were sent to other persons of distinction, including French, in spite of the war. Suzanne Curchod certainly received a copy, though whether as a gift from Gibbon is not known. A German traveller, Heinrich Matthias Marcard, afterwards learned at Geneva that Suzanne was intent on publishing a refutation of it, but was restrained by a family friend, Paul Moultou.

Replete with flourishes of erudition, but staccato in style, this first publication of Gibbon's is not unimportant as an early contribution to the history of

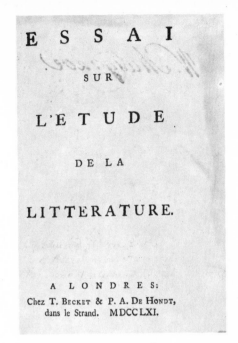

ESSAI

SUR

L'ETUDE

DE LA

LITTERATURE.

A LONDRES:
Chez T. BECKET & P. A. DE HONDT,
dans le Strand. MDCCLXI.

Gibbon's first published work

religion, and an indication of his own views on this subject. He avoided alike acceptance of divine revelation and attribution of religion to fraudulent theocracy intent on exercising temporal power. Instead, he preferred to see the origins of religion in the reactions of primitive man to phenomena he could not understand; these must have been numerous, and still are.

The search for further subjects of study and composition went on. It involved the consideration and rejection of the French expedition into Italy under Charles VIII, 'which changed the face of Europe'; the Crusade of Richard I; the Barons' War; the Black Prince and the emperor Titus; Henry V, Sir Philip Sidney, the Marquess of Montrose, and Sir Walter Raleigh. Gibbon shrank from all these, and then considered the possibility of writing on the history of the liberty of the Swiss, but this needed a knowledge of German which he lacked. Then there was the history of the republic of Florence, 'singular men and singular events'; but he was forced to ask himself when, where or how he could do it.

On 23 December 1762 the Militia was demobilized. The thirty months of service had, of course, impeded study but had not been completely wasted, for in later years Gibbon acknowledged that 'the discipline and evolutions of a modern battalion gave me a clearer notion of the phalanx and the legion, and the captain of the Hampshire grenadiers has not been useless to the historian of the Roman empire'.

The Quai Pelletier and Hôtel de Ville, Paris

The Pont Neuf, Paris, a view of 1760

Mme Geoffrin's *salon* in Paris, meeting-place of the Philosophes

Within a week of his return to civilian life, Gibbon had obtained his father's approval to go abroad for two years. On 10 February 1763 the Treaty of Paris was signed, putting an end to the Seven Years War, but Gibbon had not waited for it. He left London on 23 January, well supplied with recommendations and introductions, and five days later he arrived in Paris, on his first visit.

He took rooms on the Left Bank, at the Hôtel de Londres in the Rue du Colombier, now the Rue de l'Université, at six guineas a month. His coach cost him sixteen guineas a month, for the capital of civilization was crowded with foreign visitors on the conclusion of the war. Gibbon found that his reputation as author of the *Essai* had preceded him and served as a better introduction than many of his recommendations; he was immediately received

The Grand Tour: Paris

49

into Parisian society. He presented himself in the *salon* of Mme Geoffrin, where he met with great kindness and made the acquaintance of the flower of progressive French thought in such men as d'Alembert, Diderot, Helvétius and d'Holbach, whose talents he admired although he rejected their intolerant atheistic zeal.

Other great names in the Parisian galaxy of scholarship to whom he became known were the archaeologist Comte de Caylus, the Abbés Barthélemy, Raynal and de la Bletterie, the Academician Duclos, the Hellenist Capperonnier and La Condamine. He found that 'the society of Madame du Bocage was more soft and moderate than that of her rivals'; but his best woman friend during his stay was Mme Marie-Jeanne Bontems, who had translated Thomson's *Seasons* into French. She looked after him like a mother, accompanied him on excursions to Versailles, Saint-Germain and Saint-Denis, and allowed him to accompany her to church. The pleasures of the play at the Théâtre-Français, the Opéra, and visits to the Invalides, the Cabinet des Médailles and the Library of Saint-Germain-des-Prés, helped fourteen weeks to slip away all too swiftly, and on 9 May Gibbon left Paris to continue his Grand Tour.

Among the leading scholars Gibbon learnt to know in Paris were Claude-Adrien Helvétius, Comte de Caylus, and Abbé Raynal

Denis Diderot, the great Encyclopaedist ▶

John Baker Holroyd, afterwards Lord Sheffield,
Gibbon's lifelong friend

Lausanne a
second time
Making his way through Dijon and Besançon (where a kinsman of his,
Acton, lived), he arrived on 25 May at Lausanne, where Pavillard welcomed
him with open arms. Gibbon did not stay with him, however, but at the elegant
boarding-house run by Henri de Crousaz de Mésery, in the Rue de Bourg,
who also had a country-house a few miles away. There he found a select company of foreigners assembled; these were presently joined by John Baker Holroyd,
a war-time cavalry officer, whom Gibbon slowly got to know and appreciate,
and who was to become his greatest English friend.

A late eighteenth-century view of Lausanne, by W. Mackinnon

Many of Gibbon's fellow-lodgers were high-spirited young men who behaved riotiously in the town, and he sometimes participated. On one occasion,
after they had drunk too much, they got into trouble with the watch, and
Gibbon, as the best French-speaker among them, had to conduct the defence.
By treating the matter with a high hand and threatening to bring it before the
government in Berne, under whose absolute rule the Pays de Vaud stood, he
arranged for the affair to be settled with apologies from the Lausanne police.
This episode, together with the ceremony of the appointment by Berne of a

The city of Geneva in 1736

new Governor of Lausanne, which Gibbon attended, may have been the reason that led him to write a pamphlet harping on the total lack of political freedom from which the inhabitants of the Pays de Vaud suffered under their lords and masters of Berne. In the style of the times, he composed it in the form of a 'Letter from a Swede', addressed anonymously to an unnamed correspondent – the technique adopted by Pascal in his *Provinciales* and Montesquieu in his *Lettres persanes*, both authors with whose works Gibbon was familiar.

The 'Swede' begins by extolling the climate, soil and commerce of the Pays de Vaud. 'But I consider the people rather than their territory', he went on. It is the only country whose inhabitants, while they think freely and boldly, live politely and elegantly. 'What then is wanting: Liberty; and deprived of it, you have lost your all.' Gibbon would not have thought like this thirty years later. He went on to speak of the sovereign power in the hands of three hundred Bernese families, 'born to command' a population of 100,000 Vaudois 'doomed to submission'. He loses no opportunity of rubbing salt into the wound by showing that there is not a single useful establishment which the Pays de Vaud

owes to the sovereignty of Berne, and that unless a Vaudois belongs to the landed aristocracy the only encouragement for him is in a Swiss regiment in foreign service, where 'the ensign is ruined, the captain can scarcely live, and the colonel cannot save money'. Arrived at this point, the 'Swede' imagines his correspondent asking, 'What advice do you give us?', to which the answer is first, remonstration, and, second, 'There is another remedy, more prompt, more perfect, and more glorious. William Tell would have prescribed it. I do not', he hastens to add, thus providing himself with a typical eighteenth-century literary alibi after broaching the subject of an armed uprising. The manuscript was found among his papers after his death, and it is difficult to know how plainly Gibbon realized what political dynamite these pages contained, and what would have happened to him if they had fallen into the hands of the government.

Gibbon had not been long in Lausanne before he received a letter from Suzanne Curchod, saying that she had remained constant to him, and wanting, very reasonably, to know what his feelings were towards her now, in case she should meet him. She was now an orphan, earning her living in Geneva by

Suzanne Curchod
again

55

looking after the children of Pastor Paul Moultou, an intimate friend of Jean-Jacques Rousseau, then a refugee close by at Môtiers-Travers, in the Principality of Neuchâtel which belonged to the King of Prussia.

In a desperate attempt to effect a reconciliation between Gibbon and Suzanne, Moultou implored Rousseau to intercede with Gibbon on her behalf. Rousseau re-read Gibbon's *Essai,* thought poorly of it (Gibbon expressly rejected Rousseau's favourite and perverse claim that science and arts were the cause of all vice), and replied that as Gibbon was not his man, he could not think that he was the man for Mlle Curchod. All this was wasted effort, because, from what he had heard, Gibbon wrote to reproach her for having pretended to be miserable when she was in fact enjoying herself in Lausanne society. He went on to say that he had returned to Lausanne to study, and not to renew their engagement. To this she replied, reproaching him bitterly for concealing his real sentiments from her for so long, but offering her friendship, which Gibbon accepted. He met her by accident at supper, after a performance in Voltaire's theatre at Ferney, and on other occasions, and, as will be seen, they remained friends.

Voltaire's house at Ferney, near Geneva, where Gibbon saw a performance of
L'Orphelin de la Chine

Jean-Jacques Rousseau,
a portrait by Allan Ramsay

Gibbon spoke the truth when he said that he had come to Lausanne to study. He came to fit himself for his visit to Italy, 'a country that every Scholar must long to see'; and it was as a scholar that he prepared himself for his journey, by compiling a gazetteer of ancient geography and reading Horace, Virgil, Juvenal, Livy, Pliny, Strabo and the Antonine Itinerary. His journal was now filled with critical remarks on texts, etymology and moral judgments. While he did not deprive himself of the entertainment available in Lausanne, he refused to accompany Holroyd and his party on a tour of Switzerland, partly because it would have taken him away from his books, and partly, perhaps, because he suspected that his companions would not omit such things as a visit to the notorious brothel at Berne, so vividly described by Casanova. Instead, he waded through ponderous tomes by Renaissance scholars on Italian antiquities, numismatics and the geography of ancient Rome, to equip himself as a humanist with the necessary knowledge to appreciate the lives and works of the classical authors.

Gradually the pages of his journal widen their theme. He argues critically about the site of Virgil's tomb, the Homeric story of the Laestrygones, Hannibal's march across the Alps and the relative merits of Polybius's and Livy's accounts of it, Stilicho's victory over the Goths, the foundation of Venice and the climatic conditions of Roman civilization.

Italy In company with one of his fellow-lodgers, William Guise, Gibbon left Lausanne on 18 April 1746 on the next leg of the tour which would take him to the Promised Land. A fortnight later, after crossing Mont Cenis, they arrived at Turin, where Gibbon was introduced to the King of Sardinia, Charles-Emanuel. 'The most sociable women I have met with are the King's daughters. I chatted for about a quarter of an hour with them, . . . and grew so very free and easy, that I drew my snuff-box, rapped it, took snuff twice (a Crime never known before in the presence-chamber) and continued my discourse in my usual attitude of my body bent forward, and my fore finger stretched out.' He had painted a portrait of himself.

Milan, a visit to the Borromean Islands, 'an enchanted palace, a work of the fairies in the midst of a lake encompassed with mountains and far removed from

Crossing Mont Cenis in the Alps, 1755

58

The bridge over the Po at Turin, by Canaletto

Isola Bella, one of the Borromean Islands in Lago Maggiore

The harbour of Genoa, an eighteenth-century engraving

A view of Florence, by Thomas Patch

Sir Horace Mann, the British envoy in Florence, and his friends

the haunts of men', Genoa which disappointed him, Parma, Modena and
Bologna, and they reached Florence where they spent the three hot months of
the summer, admiring the works of art and enjoying the hospitality and protection of Sir Horace Mann, the British envoy.

On through Pisa, Lucca and Siena, and then, 'I can neither forget nor
express the strong emotions which agitated my mind as I first approached and
entered the *eternal City*.'

He had a sleepless night before he visited the Forum, and several days of
intoxication were lost or enjoyed before he could descend to a cool and minute
examination of the multitude of places hallowed by his favourite ghosts,
Romulus, Cicero and Caesar. His later autobiographical sketches contain a
number of accounts of the revelation that came to him, of which the following
is one: 'It was at Rome, on the 15th of October 1764, as I sat musing amidst
the ruins of the Capitol, while the bare-footed Fryars were singing vespers in

Rome

the Temple of Jupiter, that the idea of writing the decline and fall of that city first started on my mind.' With these famous words, the place and date of birth of his great work seem to be more firmly established than those of any other book. And yet, the matter bristles with problems.

In the first place, Gibbon wrote more than one birth-certificate for his book. Another of these runs: 'It was the view of Italy and Rome which determined the choice of the subject. In my Journal the place and moment of conception are recorded: the fifteenth of October 1764, in the close of the evening, as I sat musing in the Church of the Zoccolanti or Franciscan Fryars, while they were singing vespers in the Temple of Jupiter on the ruins of the Capitol.' So here, Gibbon was not sitting amidst the ruins, but in the Church of Santa Maria in Aracœli: such are the tricks that the passage of time and hindsight

The Forum in Rome, by Canaletto

The Capital and Church of Santa Maria in Aracoeli, Rome, by Bellotto

The Piazza del Popolo in Rome, by Piranesi

play on the memories of man. Even more curious, Gibbon's journal contains no entry of any kind, on that date or any other, of the event which, over the years, had marked itself more indelibly in his mind than on the paper of his journal; for there is no reason to doubt that 1764 was a crucial date in his career, and that he came down from the Capitoline Hill bearing the Law of his life.

A visit to Naples where he was again introduced to a king, this time by Sir William Hamilton, a return to Rome, a pilgrimage to Loretto, and the continuation of his journey to Ferrara, Venice which sadly disappointed him, 'stinking ditches dignified with the pompous denomination of canals, a fine bridge spoiled by two rows of houses on it, and a large square decorated with the worst Architecture I ever yet saw', Verona and its amphitheatre, Padua and its moribund University, Vicenza and its Palladian palaces, and a recrossing of Mont Cenis, led him back to Paris.

Canaletto's painting of the Piazzetta in Venice ▶

Eighteenth-century engraving of 'Virgil's Tomb', a short way from Naples

Georges Deyverdun

Jacques Necker

Mme Necker   During the time that he was in Italy, matters had developed in Suzanne Curchod's life. The Duchess of Grafton had thought of employing her as a governess and taking her back from Geneva to England. Fortunately for Suzanne, this did not happen. Instead, a beautiful widow, Mme Germaine de Vermenoux, engaged her as a companion and took her to Paris. Mme de Vermenoux was being courted by the banker and financier, Jacques Necker, of Geneva, established in Paris; but it was Suzanne whom he married. When Gibbon returned to Paris he found his old flame established in dignity and riches, and one of the charming parts of this astonishing true story is that whereas he previously had one friend, he now had two. 'The Curchod (Madame Necker) I saw at Paris. She was very fond of me, and the husband particularly civil. Could they insult me more cruelly? Ask me every evening to supper; go to bed, and leave me alone with his wife – what an impertinent security!'

He tore himself from Paris and, on 25 June 1765, returned to Buriton.

England again   To Gibbon's great delight, Georges Deyverdun came to England in 1765, and it was not long before the two bosom friends got together. Deyverdun

Gibbon's and Deyverdun's joint
publication, which appeared in 1768

MEMOIRES

LITTERAIRES

DE LA

GRANDE BRETAGNE,

Pour l'An 1767.

A LONDRES,
Chez T. BECKET & P. A. DE HONDT,
dans le Strand.
M DCC LXVIII.

helped Gibbon with a preliminary sketch written in French for his old cherished project of a history of the Swiss Republics, which was sent to David Hume for his comments. Hume encouraged it, but asked, as Horace did of Romans who wrote in Greek, why Gibbon carried faggots into the wood: 'our solid and increasing establishments in America . . . promise a superior stability to the English language'. Within a very few years, and under Gibbon's nose, as will be seen, the stability of 'our' establishments in America was to be completely destroyed, but the language has remained, whether 'stable' or no – although it is said that the United States narrowly avoided adopting German as its official language, so great was the hatred of everything English.

Next, Gibbon and Deyverdun collaborated in a review designed to inform Continental readers of new developments in English literature, drama and fine arts, and two volumes of *Mémoires littéraires de la Grande Bretagne* appeared in 1768 and 1769. But these publications lost money so heavily that they were discontinued. In addition, Deyverdun then abandoned the post in the Foreign Office which he owed to Hume and went abroad as a travelling tutor.

Pall Mall, London, in 1741. Gibbon lodged here when he visited London between 1770 and 1773

Gibbon turned to another subject, and on 3 February 1770 he published his first book in English: *Critical Observations on the Sixth Book of the Aeneid.* Under this cryptic and anodyne-sounding title lurked an attack on Bishop Warburton's view that Virgil's visit to the Underworld was based on the Eleusinian Mysteries. Gibbon's book was published anonymously, and he was afterwards ashamed of his cowardice.

Meanwhile, Rome continued to exert its pressure, and systematic reading continued, but everything was interrupted by the death of Gibbon's father, a merciful release from illness and blindness, on 12 November 1770, intestate.

Now in possession of his inheritance, Gibbon considered how best to dispose of his property in such a way as to further his scholarly designs. He was no countryman; he never handled a gun and seldom mounted a horse. There was therefore no question of continuing to live at Buriton. Business frequently brought him to London, where he stayed in lodgings in Pall Mall, opposite the house of the Duke of Cumberland. Holroyd had in the meantime married Abigail Way and bought Sheffield Place, near Fletching in Sussex, where

A portrait of Gibbon by Thomas Patch

Gibbon was a frequent guest and his intimate friendship with the Holroyd family began. Buriton was let, Mrs Gibbon went to live at Bath, and in January 1773 Gibbon settled in 7 Bentinck Street, a house which was to be his home for ten years.

'Decline and Fall' 'No sooner was I settled in my house and library, than I undertook the composition of the first volume of my History. At the outset all was dark and doubtful; even the title of the work, the true æra of the Decline and Fall of the Empire, the limits of the introduction, the division of the chapters, and the order of the narrative; and I was often tempted to throw away the labour of seven years. The style of an author should be the image of his mind, but the choice and command of language is the fruit of exercise. Many experiments were made before I could hit the middle tone between dull chronicle and a rhetorical declamation; three times I composed the first chapter, and twice the second and third, before I was tolerably satisfied with their effect.'

In 1775, the manuscript of the first volume was finished, but Peter Elmsley, the publisher who had brought out Gibbon's book on the *Aeneid*, was frightened of the new work. Gibbon accordingly arranged with Thomas Cadell the

7 Bentinck Street, the house where Gibbon lived from 1773 to 1783

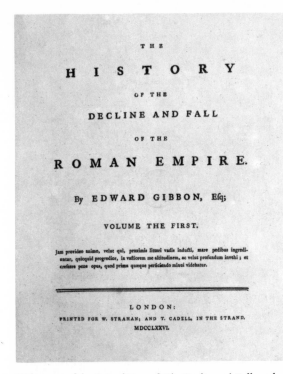
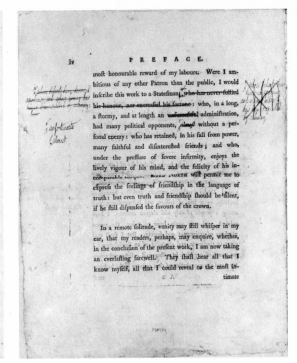

Title-page of the first edition of *The Decline and Fall*, and proof of
the Preface with Gibbon's corrections

bookseller and William Strahan the printer to publish it. At first only five
hundred copies were to have been printed, but this number was doubled, and
the first volume was published on 17 February 1776. 'A handsome quarto
costing one guinea unbound', it sold 'like a threepenny pamphlet on the affairs
of the day'. Hume and Robertson praised it highly, and Gibbon became famous
overnight: he had written the best book of all.

By its diction, music and balanced phrases, the reader is carried along at a
speed which the author controls through his masterly use of language, to suit
his meaning in different places in the text, with the help of alliteration and the
skilful use of duplicated nouns and epithets: e.g. 'the choice and command of
language'. The style is so clear that the message is conveyed not only by the
words themselves and the order in which they are introduced, but by the
pattern that Gibbon's three-member periods of phrase spell out, and a judicious
alternation between sentences long and short, so that a paragraph is a progress,
and it is never necessary to turn back to make sure that a previous sentence has
been completely understood.

Arnaldo Momigliano, a modern critic, has shown how Gibbon was poised between the humanist scholar and the historian. The antithesis between extreme holders of these points of view, already adumbrated in the *Essai,* was a reflection of the contemporary conflict between the erudite antiquarians and the philo-sophic historians, between those who thought that history was an exhaustive succession of political and military facts, collected with prodigious labour and scrupulous care, and those who conceived of history as the pageant of bar-barism and civilization, revealed in laws, customs, religious beliefs and the pattern of trade, drawn with a broad brush dipped in imagination and de-spising details which, in Voltaire's eyes, were 'the vermin that destroys great works'. In similar vein, Rousseau began his argument in the discourse on the origin of inequality between men, with the words, 'Let us then discard all the facts, for they do not bear on our problem.'

Gibbon's contribution was to integrate these two streams. He saw the necessity for making the peoples of the past live real lives, acted upon by all the strains, stresses, loves, hatreds, ambitions, satisfactions and vices that human beings are heir to, subjected to all the miseries that are their lot. But he also knew that history cannot be written without facts, and that their collection, verifica-tion and selection require erudition. History must be not only as reliable as available evidence can make it, but readable and acceptable to the general reader, not merely the learned colleague. The man of letters must be a man of taste.

He must also be a man of moral judgment, as emerges from Gibbon's definition of history as 'little more than the register of the crimes, follies, and misfortunes of mankind'. In the same vein, but more abrupt in style, a century later, Alexander Herzen defined history as the autobiography of a madman, and Tolstoy as a deaf man answering questions that nobody asked.

But in the eighteenth century the cleavage between *érudits* and *philosophes* existed, as already mentioned, and in making this synthesis Gibbon broke new ground. Far from conforming to the facile view which would make Gibbon a disciple of French eighteenth-century rationalism, he picked his way in-dependently, as Giuseppe Giarrizzo has recently shown, learning method and technique from Bayle, gathering material from Tillemont, taking a select little from Montesquieu, opposed to Voltaire, Rousseau and the *Encyclopédistes,* judiciously influenced by Hume and Robertson, and supplied by his in-exhaustible fount of knowledge, tempered by an artistry and expression all his own. It was not the work of an insular author, but of a European humanist and rhetorician.

It cannot, of course, be claimed that the *Decline and Fall* has not been over-taken by modern research in method and materials. In Gibbon's day, source

Henry Walton's portrait of
Gibbon around 1775, when he
was 37 years old and preparing
The Decline and Fall for publication

criticism was scarcely available in Britain, though German scholars, whose language he did not possess, were beginning to develop this analysis. Epigraphy at the time had but little to offer in the way of inscriptions of the second to the fifth centuries, on which much of modern knowledge of that period is based. And, steeped in the classical tradition, Gibbon had little notion of sociological evolution. What he did was to marshal the chaos of the past into intelligible order, making sense and expressing most of the ideas about civilization that were then available. He was the last of the line of historians to possess the knowledge and the ability to cover so much ground so well, in a classic masterpiece, a work of art and a product of genius. It continues to be read for its own sake. At the same time, its attribution of the fall of Rome to moral decline and to the loss of freedom, virtue and honour, is a lesson that has not lost its value.

The young Germaine Necker, daughter of Suzanne Curchod and the Director-General of the Finances of France, who became Mme de Staël (see p. 115)

Paris a second time   It must have been an added gratification to Gibbon that his triumph was witnessed by M. and Mme Necker who came to London in May 1776, accompanied by their daughter Germaine, the future Mme de Staël. In the following year, Gibbon returned the visit, and stayed in the Hôtel de Modène, in the Rue Jacob. M. Necker had become Director-General of the Finances of France. Little Germaine offered to marry Gibbon so that he could stay with them for ever.

Marquise du Deffand   Abbé de Mably

'As their friend I was introduced to the best company of both sexes: to the foreign ministers of all nations; and to the first names and characters of France.' He had supper with Mme du Deffand, was invited by the Prime Minister, the Duc de Choiseul, and was presented at Court. He consulted the Royal Library and that of the Abbey of Saint-Germain-des-Prés, and was allowed to take books home with him. He met the great Buffon, and at the home of a friend, M. de Foncemagne, he had a famous battle with the Abbé de Mably, who had satisfied himself from the study of Livy that republican systems provided the best political constitutions, and did not doubt that the historian of the decline and fall of the Roman Empire would agree with him. But Gibbon, on the contrary, spoke in favour of monarchy, and refuted Mably's argument by means of quotations from Livy and Plutarch with which he was much more familiar than his interlocutor, whose 'jealous, irascible spirit revenged itself on a work, which he was incapable of reading in the original', and in which he objected to the explanation of the causes of events about to be described.

BENJ. FRANKLIN. L.L.D.

Georges-Louis Leclerc Buffon (1707–88), the great French naturalist, who aroused Gibbon's interest in the natural sciences

Benjamin Franklin, who represented the interests of the United States in France between 1776 and 1785

Another celebrity who happened to be in France in 1777 was Benjamin Franklin, envoy from the Continental Congress in America which had just declared its independence. A story told by William Cobbett has it that the two men were in the same house, and that Gibbon, while acknowledging his admiration for Dr Franklin, could not bring himself to speak to a rebel; upon which Franklin sent a message to say that when Gibbon came to write the 'Decline and Fall of the British Empire', he would be happy to supply him with information. Apparently, however, the two did meet at dinner, and Franklin's alleged remark would not have shocked Gibbon, for his *History* contains many hints of parallels to be drawn between the Roman and British Empires.

John Hunter, lecturer in anatomy;
a portrait by Sir Joshua Reynolds

On 3 November Gibbon was back in Bentinck Street, and began to occupy himself in an unexpected manner; he attended lectures and demonstrations on anatomy by John Hunter, and on chemistry by Bryan Higgins. 'The principles of these sciences, and a taste for books of Natural History contributed to multiply my ideas and images.' One wonders whether it might not have been Buffon, a member of the Académie Française as well as of the Académie des Sciences, and no less famous as a writer than as a naturalist, who led Gibbon to take this step.

Criticism   While praise for the *Decline and Fall* continued to flow, adverse criticism began to appear, aimed at the blasphemy and immorality which some readers professed to find in the book, and especially in the fifteenth and sixteenth chapters. By associating the decay of Roman greatness with the rise of Christianity, Gibbon had brought religion into secular history on the same footing, and deprived theology of the privileged, sheltered position which it had hitherto enjoyed – a new departure in historiography.

The two chapters which raised most controversy were intended by Gibbon to show that Christianity had spread by 'natural' instead of miraculous means, and that persecution of Christians by pagans compared favourably with persecution of pagans and heretics by Christians, because of the intolerant zeal of the latter, derived from Jewish religion. Gibbon disliked intolerance, bigotry and superstition as much as Voltaire did, and his book is full of adverse criticism of the behaviour of wielders of temporal power at theological behest: 'The freedom of the mind, the source of every generous and rational statement, was destroyed by the habits of credulity and submission; and the monk, contracting the vices of a slave, devoutly followed the faith and passions of his ecclesiastical tyrant.'

It was at the door of the Church that Gibbon laid the blame for the chequered course of his own life during adolescence, and in a manuscript not published until after his death, he was even more severe, speaking of mendicant friars as 'numerous vermin . . . who disgraced religion, learning, and common sense', and of Saint Louis as a man of uncommon virtues and abilities, 'disgraced by the title of Saint'.

It was not surprising that some minds, too committed to admire and too limited to appreciate, should have attacked Gibbon as an enemy of Christianity, and this at a time when the Statute Book still contained provision for a sentence of three years in goal for whoever twice denied the truth of Christianity in writing. But Gibbon never denied the truth of Christianity; he only made some Christians, their cruelty and their verbal trickery the target for his devastating irony. It was not at religion that he tilted, but at theologians, clericalism, fanaticism and superstition.

That bigots should question his morals or his beliefs did not move him, but when his good faith was impugned, he was roused and published *A Vindication of some passages in the Fifteenth and Sixteenth Chapters of the History of the Decline and Fall of the Roman Empire*. On its appearance Horace Walpole said, 'There is, in sooth, a charming novelty today . . . an answer from Mr Gibbon to the monks that have attacked his two famous chapters. It is the quintessence of argument, wit, temper, spirit, and consequently of victory.' As for attacks on Gibbon's accuracy, Richard Porson, a classical scholar, acknowledged that he was unable to find a single instance of inaccurate quotation or deduction from sources in the whole *History*. Some years later, Henry Milman, Dean of St Paul's, closed the subject when he wrote, 'Gibbon, with a single discharge from his ponderous artillery of learning and sarcasm, laid prostrate the whole disorderly squadron' of his attackers.

It was not only Gibbon's criticisms of theology that came under attack, but his morals; and here he cannot be absolved from sailing very near impropriety,

Attacks on
The Decline and Fall

A

VINDICATION

OF

SOME PASSAGES

IN THE

Fifteenth and Sixteenth Chapters

OF THE

HISTORY of the DECLINE and FALL of
the ROMAN EMPIRE.

BY THE AUTHOR.

LONDON:
PRINTED FOR W. STRAHAN; AND T. CADELL,
IN THE STRAND.
MDCCLXXIX.

Title-page of Gibbon's *Vindication,*
published in 1779

even when concealed in footnotes in the cipher and 'obscurity of a learned language', sometimes incompletely, as in the case of the Empress Theodora. But, as he pointed out, 'her vices form an essential feature in the reign and character of Justinian'.

Nor is the text of the *Decline and Fall* free from occasional salacious remarks, as, for instance, the description of the emperor Gordian II: 'Twenty-two acknowledged concubines, and a library of sixty-two thousand volumes, attested the variety of his inclinations, and from the productions which he left behind him, it appears that the former as well as the latter were designed for use rather than ostentation.' Such passages are so full of wit, and expose with such brilliance the Emperor's New Clothes of hypocrisy, from which even the present day has not freed itself, that only very poor hearts can fail to rejoice over the fun poked in this and similar sallies. When Thomas Bowdler applied his Puritan technique to the *Decline and Fall*, 'for the Use of Families and Young Persons', the result was only a literary eunuch and a dismal failure.

The Club   By his own efforts and talents, Gibbon had established his social and scholarly position, even before the publication of the first volume of the *Decline and Fall*. A close personal friend of Oliver Goldsmith, Joshua Reynolds and David Garrick, he was already a member of the leading London clubs, such as

Sir Joshua Reynolds
(a self-portrait) and Oliver
Goldsmith, who were among
Gibbon's social circle
in London

David Garrick, a portrait by
Thomas Gainsborough

Dr Samuel Johnson, who was not
one of Gibbon's admirers

Boodle's, Brooks's and White's, when he was proposed for membership of an even more select and strictly limited body, the Literary Club, whose first recorded dinner he attended on 7 April 1775. There he consorted regularly at dinner with men like his friends just mentioned, and with Dr Johnson, Edmund Burke, George Colman, Sir William Jones, Charles James Fox, Richard Brindsley Sheridan, Charles Burney, Adam Smith, Sir Joseph Banks and James Boswell. He got on well with all of them, except Boswell and Johnson. The Great Bear (John Aubrey would have said of Gibbon and Johnson, 'surely their Mercuries are in opposition') and Gibbon kept their distance. Perhaps it did not help that Gibbon's housekeeper in Bentinck Street, Phoebe Ford, was Johnson's cousin. But Boswell hated Gibbon, and after publication of the *Decline and Fall* he, of all people, affected a high moral tone and a piety which lashed out at Gibbon for his 'infidelity'. 'Gibbon is an ugly, affected disgusting fellow, and poisons our literary club to me.' Boswell even longed for a new and different club from which Gibbon would be excluded; but it was Gibbon who founded a new club, the Romans, to which friends who had met in Italy were admitted, but not Boswell.

Gibbon's cousins, Edward Eliot and his wife, painted by Richard Wilson

It was natural that Gibbon should eventually aspire to membership of yet another club, the House of Commons. In 1774 he was working at his *History*, 'destroying an army of barbarians', when he received a visit from Edward Eliot, his cousin by marriage, the 'Cornish Lord of Boroughs', who offered him a seat. It would cost £2,400, and Eliot suggested that they should share this expense. Gibbon, whose financial position was strained, feared that he could not easily raise his share, whereupon they agreed that it should be paid in eight years' time, when Eliot's second son came of age. Gibbon did not even know which his seat would be, but a General Election was held in September 1774, and he was returned as Member for Liskeard, without having gone there, and without his constituents (who voted 'like Mr Eliot') having seen him.

Liskeard, Cornwall. Gibbon was MP for Liskeard from 1774 to 1780

Parliament

Gibbon's entry into Parliament coincided with the contest between Great Britain and the American Colonies. The Boston Tea-Party had taken place, and hostilities were soon to break out. Gibbon 'supported with many a sincere and *silent* vote the rights, though not, perhaps, the interests of the mother country'. He never spoke in the House where 'the great speakers fill me with despair, the bad ones with terror'.

The disaster of General Burgoyne's surrender at Saratoga in 1777 made Gibbon uncomfortably critical of the policies of Lord North's government, but presently he was able to render a service to the government and the nation which he, and probably nobody else, was so well fitted to perform. The quarrel between Britain and the American Colonies was, at basis, domestic, a rebellion of some of the King's subjects against their sovereign. But, as always in such events, it was not long before other Powers saw their opportunity to fish in troubled waters, and to profit by the embarrassment of Britain to gain advantage for themselves. In particular, France was supplying arms and ammunition to the rebels, in a form of undeclared war against Britain. In this widening contest, Spain began by trying to mediate, but was soon sucked into the vortex, and a declaration by the Spanish government in June 1779 constituted in effect a declaration of war. On 13 July, a reply was handed to the Spanish Ambassador, with a text in English and in French; the French text was revised by Gibbon.

EXPOSÉ

DES

MOTIFS

de la Conduite du Roi de FRANCE,
relativement à l'ANGLETERRE.

———

MÉMOIRE

JUSTIFICATIF

POUR SERVIR DE

RÉPONSE

À l'EXPOSÉ, &c.

de la Cour de FRANCE.

LONDRES:
De l'Imprimerie de T. HARRISON et S. BROOKE,
Et se vend chez P. ELMSLY, dans le Strand.

M.DCC.LXXIX.

The State Paper written
anonymously by Gibbon in 1779

The psychological warfare was intensified when, shortly afterwards, a French manifesto, entitled *Exposé des Motifs de la Conduite du Roi de France*, was issued from Paris to the Courts of Europe. Both the Lord Chancellor and the Secretary of State, Lord Weymouth, invited Gibbon to write the reply. He was given access to all the relevant papers, and the *Mémoire Justificatif pour servir de réponse à l'Exposé de la Cour de France*, written in French by Gibbon, was issued by the British government in October 1779. 'Though I will never make myself the Champion of a party, I thought there was no disgrace in becoming the Advocate of my Country against a foreign enemy, and the *Mémoire Justificatif* which you may read was the result of that opinion. The publication was delayed for various reasons, but it has now been communicated as a State Paper and in the King's name to all the Ministers and Courts of Europe.' The name of the author was not published, but the secret was easily pierced, and the *Journal Politique de Bruxelles* stated that 'it had not passed unnoticed that a bad case had been entrusted to an eloquent man.' Beaumarchais praised the style of Gibbon's *Mémoire Justificatif*, but in his reply, Gibbon said, 'the grossness of his invective betrays the loss of temper and of wit'.

Charles James Fox, one of the leading figures in Parliament during Gibbon's political career. A portrait by Sir Joshua Reynolds

R! Hon!ᵉ C.J. FOX.

The military struggle went on its dismal way, and Gibbon continued generally to vote for Lord North's disastrous policies, in spite of his misgivings, because Britain's position became so precarious that many critics rallied in support of the government. Presently, however, there was a reward, for he was appointed a Commissioner for Trade and Plantations. It was not a sinecure, for he conscientiously attended over a hundred meetings of the Board, and although it did not tax his time or his energies overduly, it represented an increase in his income of £750 a year. It may be useful to remind the modern reader that in those days Members of Parliament were unpaid. For accepting this place in spite of his privately expressed criticisms of the government, Gibbon was bitterly attacked, and particularly by Charles James Fox.

The amelioration of his financial position was very timely for Gibbon, because his other affairs, commitments and calls on his purse were not going well, and he was living above his income. He had already considered the possibility and desirability of retiring to Lausanne, but for the moment that contingency was put aside. Matters took an awkward turn when, in 1780, his patron Edward Eliot, now in Opposition, let Gibbon know that he could no longer count on his help. In the General Election of that year, Gibbon ceased to be a Member of Parliament for Liskeard. It was some consolation in November that his great friend Holroyd was elevated to the peerage as Lord Sheffield.

Early in 1781, the second and third volumes of the *Decline and Fall* were published. There were more eulogies and denunciations, with attacks by Roman Catholics which Gibbon ignored. In his *Memoirs* he merely wrote, 'The evidence of the three heavenly witnesses would now be rejected in any Court of Justice: but prejudice is blind, authority is deaf, and our vulgar Bibles will ever be polluted by this spurious text.'

A by-election returned him to Parliament on 25 June 1781 as Member for Lymington in Hampshire, which was lucky for him, as it saved his place on the Board of Trade. Gibbon then spent three months at Miss Elliot's Lodging, Cliff House, Brighton, where the air gave him health, spirits and a good appetite, and he enjoyed walking about on the Steyne and visiting bookshops.

Lymington, Hampshire, Gibbon's constituency from 1781 to 1783

The end of the Steyne in Brighton, where Gibbon lived during the summer of 1781

Hampton Court. Gibbon rented a house close by in 1782

In July 1782, by a political manœuvre cloaked as a measure of economy, the Board of Trade was abolished, and his place went with it. His seat in Parliament was now useless to him. It is remarkable that a man so learned in political history should have cut so poor a figure as a politician. It was not his element, and, as he shortly afterwards wrote to Lord Sheffield, 'the scramble for power and profit at Westminster or St James's and the names of Pitt and Fox become less interesting to me than those of Cæsar and Pompey.' That was where his heart lay.

In the autumn he rented a house from William Hamilton (who made one single speech in the House) at Hampton Court, but he had to devise a new way of living, within his income. Lord Malmesbury's letters show that Gibbon solicited a post at the British Embassy in Paris, but a passage in the third volume of the *Decline and Fall*, in which he compared Arcadius and Honorius with the slumbering occupants of the House of Bourbon, happened to catch

Benjamin Thompson (Count Rumford), who travelled with Gibbon from Dover to Boulogne in September 1783

the eye of Louis XVI, and the French government's *agrément* was not given to his appointment. In his *Memoirs* Gibbon claimed that the offending remark was written before the accession of Louis XVI and referred to his predecessors; but the damage had been done.

Inquiries of his old friend Georges Deyverdun were more than encouraging. Mme de Bochat's house at Lausanne, La Grotte, was now Deyverdun's, and he welcomed the idea of Gibbon's coming to share it with him. On 1 July 1783, Gibbon wrote to say that he was coming, and on 27 September he arrived at Lausanne.

La Grotte, the house in Lausanne that Gibbon shared with his friend
Georges Deyverdun (see p. 66)

(see p. 66)

Haven at
Lausanne
The two old bachelor friends settled in at La Grotte early in 1784, and Gibbon may be left to describe his feelings. 'I discovered three solid and per﹨ manent benefits of my new situation. 1. My personal freedom had been some﹨ what impaired by the House of Commons and the Board of Trade; but I was now delivered from the chain of duty and dependence, from the hopes and fears of political adventure; my sober mind was no longer intoxicated by the fumes of party, and I rejoyced in my escape, as often as I heard of the midnight debates which preceded the dissolution of Parliament. 2. My English oeconomy had been that of a solitary batchelor who might afford some occasional dinners. In Switzerland I enjoyed at every meal, at every hour, the free and pleasant conversation of the friend of my youth; and my daily table was always provided for one or two extraordinary guests. Our importance in society is less a positive than a relative weight: in London I was lost in the crowd; I ranked with the first families of Lausanne, and my style of prudent expence enabled me to maintain a fair balance of reciprocal civilities. 3. Instead of a small house between a street and a stable﹨yard, I began to occupy a spacious and convenient mansion, connected on the north with the City, and open on the south to a beautiful and boundless horizon. A garden of four acres had been laid out by the taste of Mr Deyverdun: from the garden a rich scenery of meadows and vineyards descends to the Leman lake, and the prospect far beyond the lake

Gibbon in his garden at
La Grotte

is crowned by the stupendous mountains of Savoy. My books and my acquaintance had been first united in London; but this happy position of my library in town *and* country was finally reserved for Lausanne. Possessed of every comfort in this triple alliance I could not be tempted to change my habitation with the changes of the season.'

All this was in refutation of the objection raised by some friends that he would not be able to exist in a Swiss town after so long conversing with the first men of the first cities of Europe. Seldom can any man have been so genuinely happy as Gibbon was, established at Lausanne with his friend, his books and his favourite madeira, obtained with the help of Lord Sheffield. Gibbon felt that he was under an obligation to the town of his choice: 'Such

A view of the city of Lausanne in 1781. The Château is on the far right, the Collège in the centre, and the Cathedral on the left.

as I am, in genius or learning or manners, I owe my creation to Lausanne: for it was in that school that the statue was discovered in the block of marble; and my own religious folly, my father's blind resolution, produced the effects of the most deliberate wisdom.'

Gibbon's reference to 'the stupendous mountains of Savoy' prompts an inquiry into his appreciation of Alpine scenery, amidst which he spent sixteen years in one of the most beautiful countries in the world. In his tour of Switzerland when he was a boy, he must have seen the Alps and the Jura every day, but never mentioned them at all. That was at a time when, as he said, 'the fashion of climbing the mountains and viewing the glaciers had not yet been introduced by foreign travellers, who seek the sublime beauties of nature'. In his later years, therefore, Gibbon must have been prepared to agree that the beauties of nature are sublime.

While he was living in Lausanne the first ascent of Mont Blanc was achieved by Dr Michel-Gabriel Paccard and Jacques Balmat, on 8 August 1786. This was a great feat, the start of the sport of mountaineering, an event sufficiently epoch-making for many Englishmen in the Alps to write home about, but there is no mention of it by Gibbon. Mont Blanc figures only twice in his

At the extreme left is the spire of the church of
St-François, behind which was Gibbon's house

writings: first in his journal on 3 April 1764 when commenting on La
Condamine's estimation of its height; and again in a note on a scrap of paper
written about 1788, in which he compared the descriptions of an eruption of
Etna given by Pindar and by Virgil, greatly to the advantage of Pindar. This
was in agreement with a principle of communication put forward by Longinus,
in which an author describes his feelings with such energy that he communicates
them to the reader. So, on reading Pindar, Gibbon writes, 'I *see* the height
of that column in the sky (which, however, is only two thirds as high as
Mont Blanc); that summit, foster-nurse of snow, the black shadow of forests,
those fountains of pure fire that emerge from it and wind into rivers of smoke and
flame; I *hear* the din of the falling, burning rocks, hurled into the deep plain
of the sea.' Gibbon sees the mountain through Pindar's eyes, not his own, and
Mont Blanc serves only as a standard of height with which to measure that of
Etna. His appreciation of mountain scenery was purely classical, and serves
better than anything else to show what a stranger he was to everything touching
the Romantic movement. But he did give very bad marks to Saint Bernard
for failing to notice 'the beauties of that incomparable landscape' when he rode
by the Lake of Geneva without seeing it.

Portrait of Dr Auguste Tissot,
by Angelica Kauffmann

Château Gibbon   The two bachelors respected each other's privacy scrupulously, and met for meals and conversation. Gibbon's time was regulated with meticulous precision, as was described by the German poet Friedrich von Matthisson: 'The most rigid punctuality reigns in his house. His servants must accomplish their allotted tasks to the minute, in accordance with the time-table, on pain of dismissal. He himself sets the example. His day is divided like that of the Saxon King Alfred. To the chime of the clock he settles down to work, sits down to dinner, or goes into society, and never spends one minute more at each of these occupations than is allowed for in his time-table. A hair-dresser was dismissed because he arrived a few minutes after seven o'clock. His successor took the precaution of coming a little early, only to receive the same fate. The third, who crossed the threshold of the door as the clock struck, was retained.' With equal precision, well or ill, Gibbon took medicine on the first day of every month.

Madame de Staël, by Isabey

What Voltaire had been at Ferney, what Mme de Staël was to become in the Rue du Bac and at Coppet, Gibbon became at Lausanne, and his modesty suffered. On 22 October 1784, he wrote to Lady Sheffield: 'A few weeks ago, as I was walking on our terrace with Dr Tissot, the celebrated physician, Mr Mercier the author of the *Tableau de Paris*; the Abbé Raynal, Monsieur, Madame, and Mademoiselle Necker, the Abbé de Bourbon a natural son of Lewis the fifteenth, the Hereditary Prince of Brunswick, Prince Henry of Prussia, and a dozen Counts, Barons, and extraordinary persons, among whom was a natural son of the Empress of Russia; are you satisfied with this list?'

It would have done Gibbon no harm to have known what Germaine Necker thought of him about this time. 'When I look at him, I ask myself if I should ever have sprung from a union between him and my mother. I say to myself, no, and that my father was sufficient for me to have come into the world.'

Sketches of Gibbon by
Lady Spencer

A member of the exclusive Cercle de Bourg, on good terms with the Bernese Bailiff of Lausanne, Baron von Erlach, Gibbon enjoyed general esteem but he was also the butt of humorous stories at his expense. One of these was that he went out every day riding on horseback, a rather cruel jest when it is realized that he suffered from an infirmity which made such an exercise quite out of the question, as will be seen. Another story was that he had become so in⁄fatuated with a lady that he fell on his knees before her and declared his passion.

Isabelle de Polier
(Mme de Crousaz), who
became Baronne de Montolieu

She declined him and desired him to rise, upon which he admitted that he
was incapable of doing so, and the lady rang for a servant and ordered him to
raise M. Gibbon. This story was probably based on the fondness that Gibbon
had shown for Mme de Crousaz, Isabelle de Polier, the widowed daughter of
that Polier de Bottens who had readmitted Gibbon to the Protestant communion
thirty years before.

In August 1785, the London newspapers reported that Gibbon had died,
a report which gave him great amusement as he read it at breakfast, and it
provides a good example of his sense of fun, as expressed in a letter to Lord
Sheffield. 'The hope of the Newswriter is very handsome and obliging to the
historian yet there are several weighty reasons which would incline me to believe
that the intelligence may be true. *Primo* it must one day be true, and therefore
may very probably be so at present. *Secundo* We may always depend on the
impartiality, accuracy and veracity of an English newspaper. *Tertio* which is

The pavilion and terrace of Gibbon's house in Lausanne

indeed the strongest argument, we are credibly informed that for a long time past, the said celebrated historian has not written to any of his friends in England and as that respectable personnage had always the reputation of a most exact and regular correspondent it may be fairly concluded that either he is or ought to be dead.'

Completion of the 'Decline and Fall'

'It was on the day or rather the night of the 27th of June, 1787, between the hours of eleven and twelve that I wrote the last lines of the last page in a summer-house in my garden. After laying down my pen, I took several turns in a *berceau* or covered walk of acacias which commands a prospect of the country the lake and the mountains. The air was temperate, the sky was serene; the silver orb of the moon was reflected from the waters, and all Nature was silent. I will not dissemble the first emotions of joy on the recovery of my freedom and perhaps the establishment of my fame. But my pride was soon humbled, and a sober melancholy was spread over my mind by the idea that I had taken my everlasting leave of an old and agreeable companion, and that, whatsoever might be the future date of my history, the life of the historian must be short and precarious.'

Gibbon's imparting of a personality to his *History* introduces the interesting relation between an author and his work. Experienced authors know that however carefully the plans of a forthcoming work may be laid down, and the general lines of literary strategy determined, it often happens that, after a certain time, the book itself takes charge, imposes its tactics on the strategy and forces the author to continue and complete it in a direction different from that originally envisaged. In Gibbon's case it seems that at the start there was no overall plan; he did not know when he began to what date he would carry on his *History*. He admitted that he had 'begun to print the head before the tail was quite finished' in the first volume; and as for the arrangement of his material, 'it was not till after many designs and many tryals, that I preferred, as I still prefer, the method of grouping my picture by nations'. The fact that he rewrote his first chapter three times, and the second and third chapters twice,

Gibbon and Lord Sheffield; silhouettes taken in 1791, when the Sheffield family visited Gibbon in Lausanne

THE HISTORIAN.   THE PEER.

John Street, Adelphi, address of
Osborne's Hotel where Gibbon stayed
during his visit to London in 1787

Wedgwood medallion of Gibbon,
about 1787

shows that it took him some time to find the style, scale and manner in which he
intended to continue. But from that moment on, his book and he were in
perfect agreement, and it is this harmony that resulted in the quality of the
masterpiece.

Armed with the precious manuscript of his last three volumes, Gibbon left
Lausanne on 29 July 1787, and reached London on 7 August, where he stayed
at Osborne's Hotel in John Street, Adelphi.

Triumph

The same arrangements as before were made with Cadell and Strahan. The
rough manuscript, which he had shown to nobody, without any intermediate
fair copy, was sent to press on 15 August. The work of proof-correcting went on
while Gibbon stayed in London at Lord Sheffield's house in Downing Street,
or at Sheffield Place, or at Bath.

The de Sévery family, Gibbon's
great friends at Lausanne.
Salomon de Charrière de Sévery
(right); his wife (right above);
and their son Wilhelm (above),
who was adopted by Gibbon

Bath in the eighteenth century, a favourite resort of Gibbon, where his stepmother lived

Gibbon had invited his young friend Wilhelm de Sévery, son of his great friends at Lausanne, Salomon and Catherine de Sévery, to come to England where he looked after him like a father, introduced him and took him round to launch him in English society, with visits to Lord North, Lord Loughborough, Lord Ossory, Sir Joshua Reynolds, the Misses Berry, the Royal Academy Banquet and the Queen's Picture Gallery and Library. Lord Glenbervie has recounted Gibbon's attendance at a *levée* when George III greeted him with the words, 'How do you do, Mr Gibbon? Always *scribble, scribble, I suppose.*' Gibbon also attended dinners of the Royal Society Club and the Literary Club, where he met many old friends and Boswell.

THE
Luminous Historian.

London; Published by W.ᵐ Holland Printseller. N.º 50,
Oxford Street, August the 12.ᵗʰ 1788.

Caricature of Gibbon in
hunting costume. The legend
'Luminous Historian' is a skit
on Sheridan's eulogy of
Gibbon at the trial of
Warren Hastings

On his fifty-first birthday, 8 May 1788, the fourth, fifth and sixth volumes
of the *Decline and Fall* were published, and his great work was completed. A
dinner was held in Thomas Cadell's house to celebrate the event at which
William Hayley sang the praise of the historian in an 'elegant compliment'. In
the following month the trial of Warren Hastings began in Westminster Hall,
and Sheridan, in his speech for the prosecution, said that 'nothing equal in
criminality was to be traced either in ancient or modern history, in the correct
periods of Tacitus or the luminous page of Gibbon'. Gibbon was present and
was afterwards teased that what Sheridan had said was 'voluminous page'.

Sheffield Place, Sussex, seat of Gibbon's friend Lord Sheffield

In taking leave of the *Decline and Fall*, we should note that Gibbon founded no school, but his influence was widespread. In a general way it is reflected in the works of those of his successors who allied history with literature. His style has been recognized in pronouncements by Winston Churchill. In another direction, his use of sarcasm mixed with simplicity amounted to what would now be called a technique of psychological warfare; Joseph Priestley had called it 'the language of deceit without deceiving'; and T. J. B. Spencer has shown how Charles Lyell was led by it to appreciate the importance of avoiding frontal attacks on received opinions, a technique which Lyell imparted to Darwin.

Parting from Lord Sheffield and his family was a wrench, but Gibbon tore himself away, and left Dover on 21 July 1788. His route this time was a variant, from Calais through Douai, La Fère, Chalons, Vimory, Gray and Pontarlier to Lausanne, where he arrived on the 30th.

Gibbon sketched in 1791 with his friend Madame de Silva

Shortly after his return, Gibbon was delighted by a visit from Charles
James Fox, with whom old scores had been made up. But before long his life
was saddened by the death of Georges Deyverdun. The good friend had made
provision for Gibbon to occupy La Grotte during the remainder of his life.
Consolation was to be found in visits to his friends, the de Séverys and the Neckers,
and great was the rejoicing when he learned that Lord and Lady Sheffield,
with their daughters Maria Josepha and Louisa, were to visit him at Lausanne
in the summer of 1791.

In the following year, however, matters across the lake were going from bad
to worse. Gibbon had begun by welcoming the reform of abuses promised
by the French Revolution, and he had comforted himself and his readers with
the conclusion that 'Europe is secure from any future irruption of barbarians;
since, before they can conquer, they must cease to be barbarous.' Yet here was
barbarism in the heart of Europe, without any migration of peoples or invasion.

Lady Sheffield, first wife of
Gibbon's closest friend

The King of France had tried to escape but had been caught, imprisoned and
deposed. Lausanne was full of French refugees, who were not well appreciated.
One of them, the Marquise de la Tour du Pin, said that Gibbon was so ugly
that she had refrained with difficulty from bursting into laughter at the sight
of him. The world was tottering, and Gibbon laid in a little store of gold, and
had two good horses ready, in case he should have to cut and run for it before
the *sans-culottes*.

Yet the year 1792 was something of an Indian summer for Gibbon. The
adulation which his genius merited served, unfortunately, to increase his
vanity – not uncommon with small and ugly men, particularly when afflicted
with an unfortunate physical ailment. The testimony of visitors to Lausanne
is therefore highly critical of him, but of value because of its impartiality. Thus
John Owen: 'Gibbon is the grand monarque of literature at Lausanne: I have
seen, conversed, and dined with him. These are, I think, the three requisites

Château Ballival, the residence in Lausanne of Gibbon's friend, Baron von Erlach, Bailiff of Berne

in order to know something of a man. His conversation is correct and eloquent; his periods are measured, and his manner of delivering them solemn. He appears rather inditing to an amanuensis, than holding conversation to a stranger. But though he talks too oracularly, he is at his table cheerful, frank, and convivial. His hospitalities are however not strictly patriotic: his predilection for the Swiss is notorious; and, as a love of pre-eminence may not be classed among the least of his failings, he seems to have decided well in the choice of his society.'

In confirmation of this, Charles Byam Wollaston found that 'Gibbon is not attentive to the English unless they are particularly recommended to him', for which he can hardly be blamed.

Portrait of Gibbon in 1781, by George Romney

Lionel Colmore: 'Mr Gibbon would never forgive me if I omitted mentioning him. I procured an admittance to him in the morning, which is a great distinction; but I did not at all enjoy his society, as the hereditary prince of Cassel was there, with two tutors and two professors, who are doing their best to make a goose of him. Gibbon is very fond of having a sort of court about him, and has frequent assemblies; at one of them I assisted, . . . all the world was there.'

Lady Holland recounted that when Gibbon attended a reception in someone else's house, everybody rose as he entered and did not sit until he had sat down. In Gibbon's own house, a reception clearly carried with it a great deal of mystique. The effusive Marie-Sophie van La Roche described one in hyperbolic terms. 'Although he has taken root in Lausanne, Gibbon preserves grand English manners, such as that of assembling a select company in his library where, as the saying goes, great friends among the dead mingle with the living.' This does not strike one as a peculiarly English custom, and it applies far better to Gibbon's librarian, David Levade, in whose house, she said, fixed to the wall beneath a picture of the tomb of the Scipios, was a human bone from the sarcophagus of Scipio Africanus. She would have liked to see Gibbon's face when he first saw it.

The great event of 1792 was the arrival at Lausanne of Georgiana, Duchess of Devonshire, her sister Lady Harriet Duncannon, their mother Lady Spencer

◀ Georgiana, Duchess of Devonshire,
by Thomas Gainsborough

Caricature of Gibbon,
attributed to Lady Diana Beauclerk

Lady Elisabeth Foster, afterwards Duchess of Devonshire, by Angelica Kauffmann (detail)

and Lady Elisabeth Foster. Gibbon was in his element; and he had much to tell them. He had called on the Neckers at Rolle shortly after the massacre of the Swiss Guards in the Tuileries on 10 August, and learned that their daughter, now Baronne de Staël-Holstein, wife of the Danish Ambassador in Paris, who had worked as a very effective female Scarlet Pimpernel in getting her friends out of France, was for the first time in her life frightened. She even tried to enlist Gibbon's support to influence Baron von Erlach to grant asylum to her protégés. All this and much more, Gibbon related to his English guests. The

Madame de Staël and her daughter Albertine, afterwards duchesse de Broglie

Duchess's letters to her daughter reveal a fresh aspect of Gibbon, his playing with the daughters of Lady Harriet Duncannon (the future Lady Caroline Lamb) and of Lady Elisabeth Foster (the future Mrs George Lamb). 'Mr Gibbon is very fond of the two Carolines – and Caroline Ponsonby does what she will with him – he is very clever but remarkably ugly and wears a green jockey cap to keep the light from his eyes.' In his *Memoirs* Gibbon frequently referred to his care to save his eyes by not working at night, and his spectacles have since been discovered; he was far-sighted.

The great ladies had taken a house at Ouchy, called l'Élysée, and there, one day, came Thomas Whaley who had been to call on William Beckford at Evian, across the lake. After the homosexual scandal in which Beckford had been involved with young Courtnay, he had consistently lived out of England. Gibbon remarked that 'it was astonishing any Englishman would visit a man who lay under such an imputation as B[eckford] did; that even supposing him innocent, still some regard was due to the opinion of the world'. Whaley replied appropriately that it was a pity that so small a matter should trouble so great an historian.

The most severe criticism of Gibbon came from Sir Charles Blagden, a great man of science and Secretary of the Royal Society, of which Gibbon had been elected a Fellow. 'Called on Mr Gibbon: very affected, not civil to me . . . grew more so afterwards. . . . Walked in Mr Gibbon's garden, talked with him some time, perfect work of art; piques himself on his fashion evidently: not great mind . . . too much like acting, as if had studied his part.'

It is a pity to have to record these opinions, but they are honest criticisms of a man who had become spoilt by public acclaim and private vanity. As far as his work is concerned, genius is in no need of whitewash.

The Duchess and her party left, and before the year was out the French Revolutionary armies had invaded Savoy, so that only the waters of the lake separated Gibbon from the new barbarians. Soon they threatened to invade and conquer Geneva, and Lausanne passed an anxious winter. When Louis XVI was executed in January 1793, Gibbon contemplated going into mourning. The champion of freedom and liberty of the *Decline and Fall*, the enemy of bigotry and intolerance, both religious and anti-religious, had become converted into a complete reactionary who even found something to be said for the Inquisition.

On 3 April 1793, Lady Sheffield died, and as soon as Gibbon received the news, although he had made it a rule for himself never to stir more than ten miles from Lausanne, he decided at once to return to England to be with his old and bereaved friend. Whatever criticism can legitimately be levelled at Gibbon for his pompous behaviour, he never allowed the bonds of friendship to weaken. He was persuaded to delay his departure for one day, solely to spend it with his friends the de Sévery family. He left Lausanne for the last time on 10 May 1793.

The journey to England was greatly complicated by the war which had now been declared between France and Britain. The usual short route was impossible, and he made for Berne and Schaffhausen. Past Karlsruhe, at Frankfurt, the sound of gunfire from the siege of Mayence could be heard. By way of Cologne and Brussels he reached Ostend with astonishing good

The last lap

William Beckford, by John Hoppner

luck, for Belgium, which then belonged to Austria, had been conquered by the French at the end of 1792, and retaken by the Austrians early in 1793. A year later it was reconquered by the French, so Gibbon slipped through just in time to avoid the detested *sans-culottes*. He arrived in London on 3 June 1793 and went straight to his friend Lord Sheffield, at his house in Downing Street.

The summer was spent at Sheffield Place, where a number of guests called and stayed, including Lord Glenbervie, Frederick North, Thomas Bowdler and Arthur Young. In October Gibbon stayed at the Cork Street Hotel in London before starting on a round of visits, to his step-mother at Bath and to Lord Spencer at Althorp. But in November he was obliged to return to London, to lodgings that he had taken at 76 St James's Street, at the corner of Little St James's Street.

Illness   On 11 November 1793, Gibbon wrote to Lord Sheffield, 'I must at length undraw the veil before my state of health. . . . Have you never observed through my inexpressibles a large prominency circa genitalia. It was a swelled testicle which as it was not at all painful, and very little troublesome, I had strangely neglected for many years.' It was thirty-two years, to be precise. He went on to tell his friend that, the day before, he had consulted the surgeon Walter Farquhar, because he had now become heavily incommoded by the recent enlargement of his tumour. The poor man affected to fancy that nobody had noticed his trouble, and Lord Sheffield found out from Gibbon's servant that his master would never tolerate any mention of his condition. Yet, at Lausanne, the surgeon Étienne Mathieu had noticed it before 1786, and said that it was a hydrocele which a puncture would reduce, but only with the prospect of its recurrence in six months.

When Gibbon returned to England in 1787, Lord Sheffield was deeply shocked at the enlargement which Gibbon's tumour had undergone, and as he had not seen him since 1783, this means that he had observed it even before that date. In 1788, the Venezuelan patriot Francisco de Miranda had noticed the disorder and the fact that it impeded Gibbon's gait.

In 1790 Gibbon, who had become extremely corpulent, began to suffer from swollen ankles, until about October 1793, when the tumour became so much enlarged that he felt at last obliged to seek medical advice. The ankle swellings became reduced at the same time.

On looking back into Gibbon's life, one finds that in 1761, when serving in the Militia, he consulted the surgeon Caesar Hawkins, who considered that the trouble must have been the start of either a hernia or a hydrocele, but could not determine which, although he inclined towards the latter view. 'He desired me to have patience till it became larger and fuller', and to return and consult him again. This Gibbon failed to do; but on 6 September 1761, when at

St James's Street, London. Gibbon died at No. 76 on 15 January 1794

Southampton he consulted a surgeon of that town, Mr Andrews, 'in relation to a complaint I had neglected for some time; it was a swelling in my left testicle which threatens being a serious affair.' Military service, as modern service-men taken from civilian life know, is a frequent source of hernial trouble. For thirty-two years after that date, there is no mention in Gibbon's *Memoirs*, journals or letters concerning this matter, although after his return to Lausanne in 1783 he restricted his outings to distances under ten miles from the town; travelling must have been painful.

Walter Farquhar was uncertain in his diagnosis because the tumour was so large, and he called in his colleague Henry Cline. Both thought that they had to deal with a hydrocele, but they wanted yet another opinion before operating on their famous patient, so Matthew Baillie was called in, and it was decided to make a puncture in the tumour to evacuate the fluid that it obviously contained, and so reduce it.

On 14 November 1793 the operation was performed, eight pints of a clear watery fluid were drawn off, and the tumour was reduced to half its size. Lord Sheffield, who was present, recounted how 'the three medical gentlemen who attended him will recall his pleasantry, even during the operation'. The terms of Gibbon's 'pleasantry' have been preserved in a letter written by Timothée Francillon, a standing guest at Sheffield Place, Pastor of the French congregation of Saint-Jean, Spitalfields in London, to David Levade, Gibbon's great friend and librarian at Lausanne. Everybody there was anxiously waiting for news. Gibbon's joke took the form of a riddle: 'Why is a fat man like a Cornish Borough?' Answer: 'Because he never sees his member.'

This typical eighteenth-century jest was true in at least two senses. First, Gibbon himself, as Member of Parliament for Liskeard, had never been seen by his constituents. Secondly, his corpulence had obstructed his view of his own anatomy. A passage in Lady Holland's journal, which Lord Ilchester omitted from his edition, describes the effects of Gibbon's affliction. She disliked Gibbon, whom she had last seen at Sheffield Place in December 1793, but there is no reason to suspect her of falsifying her observations, although they were written later. The passage runs as follows: 'A comical observation of Gibbon's in his *Memoirs* just occurs. He says, "The year 1770 was particularly favourable to the growth of my *intellectual* stature." The expressions are uncommonly ludicrous, combining it with the recollection of his misshapen, grotesque figure; for he was a monster, and so filthy withal that one could not endure being close to him. He was buttoned up in the morning, and never *opened* till he was undressed at night; thus every besoin of nature was performed in his cloaths.'

What he must have suffered in self-respect, quite apart from physical discomfort, is hard to imagine; but this disclosure shows that his friends were remarkably tolerant.

Very quickly, fluid began to collect again in Gibbon's tumour, and on 24 November 1793 a second puncture was made, and six pints of fluid were withdrawn. Gibbon seemed to be relieved after this operation, and resumed his normal mode of life, with visits to the country, social activities and dinner-parties. He returned to Sheffield Place where Maria Josepha Holroyd noted, 'Poor historian! He has been very indifferently since yesterday se'en night. It

Maria Josepha Holroyd,
Lord Sheffield's
'irrepressible' daughter

is a great effort to him going up and down stairs.' Presently he developed fever, fluid collected again, and on 7 January 1794 he returned to 76 St James's Street where, on the 13th, a third puncture was carried out and twelve pints of fluid were drawn off.

The surgeons pronounced themselves satisfied with his condition, and on their assurance Lord Sheffield left London. On the 14th Lady Spencer and Lady Lucan called on him; on the 15th he received John Craufurd of Auchenames and told him that he thought he was good for ten, twelve or perhaps twenty years. He had plans for how he would occupy himself. For dinner he ate the wing of a chicken and drank three glasses of madeira. Next day, 16 January, he awoke with more energy than he had felt for some time. Abdominal pain then set in, and with only his servant present, peaceful in mind and in full possession of his mental faculties, Gibbon died.

Fletching Church, Sussex, where Gibbon was buried

He was buried on 23 January 1794, in Fletching Church, near Sheffield Place, in the north transept, which had been set aside for the family tomb of the Sheffields.

The sad news was received by Mme Necker at Coppet, not long before she herself died, but she had the satisfaction of knowing that Gibbon had spoken the truth when he had said, so many years before, that Suzanne Curchod was the only woman whom he could marry.

So ended a life of fifty-six years, the first and last quarters of which were marred by distressing bodily ailments, while the intervening period was chequered by all sorts of interruptions: religious accidents, enforced displacements, thwarted love, military service, financial difficulties and a disappointing parliamentary career. Yet fortitude never abandoned the ugly, cheerful little man who, all by himself, achieved the highest pinnacle of literary fame and contributed more to life and the pleasure of others than he got from it.

Sir Joseph Banks,
President of the Royal
Society, friend of Gibbon
and Lord Sheffield; a
portrait by Thomas Phillips

On the Thursday before and on the Thursday after Gibbon died, Lord Sheffield dined with the Royal Society Club as the guest of Sir Joseph Banks, the President. Banks had known Gibbon very well for twenty years, and had witnessed one of Gibbon's wills. As President of the Royal Society, Banks pressed Walter Farquhar for details of the cause of Gibbon's death, not only for personal reasons, but also in the name of science, 'to satisfy the curiosity of those who ask me by what road it was he went to heaven'. The explanation given by the surgeons was wide of the mark, as was inevitable before the days of Pasteur and Lister. (Details of Gibbon's medical case history will be found in an Appendix on p. 129.)

'The road by which he went to heaven'

As Gibbon's executor, there was one more task for Lord Sheffield to perform for his friend, the editing and publication of his remaining papers. Foremost among these were the six autobiographical sketches which Gibbon wrote between 1788 and 1793. These fragments, written in different styles, on different scales, of different lengths and covering different portions of his life, formed no book as they stood. In the most skilful manner Lord Sheffield, perhaps helped by his daughter Maria Josepha, selected passages here and there, sewed them together, and produced a text that has become a vulgate and a classic. In performing his difficult task, however, Lord Sheffield took great liberties with the text, omitting some passages, deliberately changing others and running others together, in a manner that would be regarded by a modern editor as unpardonable.

The Memoirs of the Life of Edward Gibbon with various observations and excursions by himself, together with a number of separate essays found in manuscript among his papers, some letters and some minor works already published, were issued by Lord Sheffield in 1796 under the title *Miscellaneous Works of Edward Gibbon* in two quarto volumes. An enlarged octavo edition was published in 1815 (although the date on the title-page is 1814). It was well received: a reviewer referred to Gibbon as 'this enchanting writer', and added that the memoirs of his life were 'perhaps the best specimen of autobiography in the English language'.

Gibbon's most treasured possessions were his books, and the tools of his trade are so very much a part of a man and his work, that no account of his life would be complete without mention of their fate. He directed that they should be sold and they have been dispersed all over the world, but the catalogue which Sir Geoffrey Keynes has reconstructed of the library makes it possible to trace the main lines of their history.

Many accounts of their fate are so fantastic as to be absurd. Their purchaser was William Beckford, whom Gibbon had disliked, and some of Beckford's biographers have made confusion worse confounded by saying that he bought them in 1793 (when Gibbon was still alive), or in 1794 (when Beckford was in Portugal). Maria Josepha Holroyd said in 1794 that the library had been moved out of Gibbon's house as the new owner did not 'suffer it to remain there any longer'. It was in 1796 that Beckford bought the collection, as he said, 'to have something to read when I passed through Lausanne. I shut myself up for six weeks from early in the morning until night, only now and then taking a ride. The people thought me mad. I read myself nearly blind.'

The books were under the care of Dr Frédéric Scholl, who negotiated the purchase for Beckford with Gibbon's executor in London. Further information was obtained by the indefatigable Meredith Read, who learned from Mlle Fanny Scholl, daughter of the doctor, that Beckford took eight or ten volumes

Dr Frédéric Scholl

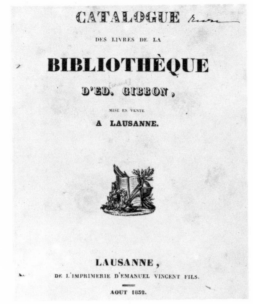

CATALOGUE

DES LIVRES DE LA

BIBLIOTHÈQUE

D'ED. GIBBON,

MISE EN VENTE

A LAUSANNE.

LAUSANNE,
DE L'IMPRIMERIE D'EMANUEL VINCENT FILS.

AOUT 1832.

Catalogue of the sale
of Gibbon's library, 1832

back to England with him and left the remainder under the care of her father. This must have been before 1797, in which year the Comte de Vaublanc visited Dr Scholl in his house at 20 Rue de Bourg and found that his books were already in his custody. Mary Berry saw them in 1802 and said that Beckford had paid £950 for them. As late as 1818, Beckford had still not removed them, for Henry Matthews then visited Lausanne and wrote, 'Gibbon's library still remains, but it is buried and lost to the world. It is the property of Mr Beckford and lies locked up in an uninhabited house at Lausanne.'

Shortly after this date, Beckford made a present of the books to Scholl, who in 1825 divided the library into two parts. He sold one half to John Walter Halliday, an Englishman then living in an old ruined castle, Les Clées, near Vallorbe. The other half was put up for sale in Lausanne by Scholl in 1831 and 1832, and bought partly by the Cantonal Library of Lausanne and partly by purchasers in Germany and the United States. Halliday took his moiety with him after he moved from Les Clées to Satigny near Geneva where, after his death, it passed into the hands of Charles Bedot. When his son, Maurice Bedot, died in 1927, that half of Gibbon's library also came into the market. A bookseller of Geneva wanted something like £4,000 for it, and Magdalen College, which was interested in purchasing it, was advised that the sum demanded was too high. As no other purchaser offered, the books made their way to England and into the catalogue of Sotheby and Co., who auctioned them on 20 December 1945. They fetched £1,577 10s. 0d.

A specimen of Gibbon's handwriting

From time to time, Gibbon's books turn up in sales, as, on 19 October 1953, Beckford's own copy of the *Decline and Fall* did at Christie's. It contained a note written by Beckford, which is worth quoting as an example of human fallibility and a warning to jealous haters. 'The time is not far distant, Mr Gibbon, when your most ludicrous self-complacency, your numerous, and sometimes apparently wilful mistakes, your frequent distortion of historical Truth to provoke a gibe, or excite a sneer at every thing most sacred and venerable, your ignorance of the oriental languages, your limited and far from acutely critical knowledge of the Latin and the Greek, and in the midst of all the prurient and obscene gossip of your notes – your affected moral purity perking up every now and then from the corrupt mass like artificial roses shaken off in the dark by some Prostitute on a heap of manure, your heartless scepticism, your unclassical fondness for meretricious ornament, your tumid diction, your monotonous jingle of periods, will be still more exposed and scouted then they have been. Once fairly knocked off from your lofty, bedizened stilts, you will be reduced to your just level and true standard. W.B.'

There are persons, like Beckford, by whom it is no disadvantage to be disliked.

A place of pilgrimage

When Gibbon died, Great Britain was engaged in a war with France which was to continue for twenty more years, except for a brief interlude in 1802. Switzerland itself was safe for Englishmen until 1798, and in the previous year Mr Arbuthnot left Lausanne and reported to the Sheffields that Gibbon's terrace, garden and acacias remained much as they were, but neglected. In 1802 his house was a goal for pilgrims who had read his recently published *Memoirs* and wanted to make personal contact with the home of the great man. In that year, W. J. MacNevin wrote: 'Every reader of English will enquire for the charming residence of Gibbon. I paid my homage there to genius, taste, and industry.' In the same year, J. G. Kemaistre visited Gibbon's house several times, met many of his old friends and recorded that 'the inhabitants of Lausanne to whom he was well known during his long residence among them, do justice to his literary reputation; but they speak of him as a man with still greater praise.' After the resumption of hostilities in 1803, Francis Kinloch of South Carolina was able to walk on Gibbon's terrace, but no Englishmen.

After the fall of Napoleon in 1814, British travellers rushed to the Continent, and among them was Samuel Rogers who said, 'at Lausanne my sister and I went to see Gibbon's house; and, borrowing the last volume of the *Decline and Fall*, we read the concluding passages of it on the very spot where they were written.' Similarly Sir James Mackintosh: 'We ran to Gibbon's house. We went into "La Gibbonnière", the little summer-house where he wrote his history, which is now somewhat dilapidated.'

Two years later, Gibbon's house received its two most distinguished pilgrims, Shelley and Byron. Shelley wrote: 'We were shewn the decayed summer-house where he finished the History, and the old acacias on the terrace, from which he saw Mont Blanc [he did not] after writing the last sentence. There is something grand and even touching in the regret which he expresses at the completion of his task.' And Byron wrote to John Murray: 'I enclose you a sprig of Gibbon's acacia and some rose leaves from his garden, which, with part of his house, I have just seen. . . . The garden and the summer-house, where he composed, are neglected, and the latter utterly decayed: but they still show it as his "cabinet".' In the following year, 1817, however, Robert Southey, Poet Laureate, was refused admittance to the garden because access to it lay through a room where somebody was ill. Frances Jane Carey had better luck: 'Monsieur was so obliging as to take us to the house where Gibbon resided, and point out to us the little summer-house in which he mentions that he finished his history.'

Gibbon's garden was accessible to Sir Egerton Brydges in 1819, and in the following year Edward John Trelawney relates that he saw his friend, the bookseller of Lausanne, 'sitting under the acacias on the terrace in front of the house in which Gibbon had lived, and where he wrote "The Decline and Fall". He said, "I am trying to sharpen my wits in this pungent air which gave such a keen edge to the great historian, so that I may fathom this book". It was Shelley's "Queen Mab".'

Gibbon's house made its way into the guide-books, and it figures in the first edition of Murray's *Handbook for Travellers in Switzerland* as something that should not be missed, but it was admitted that a new summer-house had taken the place of the old. Details of this substitution are given by Meredith Read, who heard from the lips of an old lady who had lived in the house from 1802 until 1831 the sad story of the fate of the summer-house. 'At the beginning of this period Gibbon's pavilion was still intact. But, as every English visitor cut away a portion, the historian's sanctum gradually disappeared from Lausanne, and was distributed in fragments throughout Great Britain. The family, owners of the property, strove to moderate this archaeological enthusiasm, and save the remains. Bit by bit they renewed the structure, fighting against unrelenting attacks; but eventually, like the knife of Janot, or Rabelais's robe, not a morsel of the original was left. The real had given way to a copy; but even this was destined in its turn to fall before the insatiable tourist. Finding in fact that the thirst of travellers for these relics continued unabated, the family, in utter despair, allowed the last remnant of the re-erected structure to take its flight beneath the cloak of a particularly greedy sight-seer. A little later, the guides of parties to this spot, began to point out the venerable Madame Grenier, if she chanced to be in the garden, as the widow of Gibbon.'

That this account is in no way exaggerated is clear from the conversation which Charles Pack overheard between two Englishwomen on a steamer at Ouchy in 1856. 'Ah! poor Gibbon! he wrote the Decline and Fall; but that proving a bad speculation, he set up this hotel. It was here that he fell in love with a beautiful lady called Julie, but a young Frenchman called Rousseau cut him out.'

More prosaic, but not necessarily more authentic, was the relic that Sir Charles Bunbury found at the Hôtel Gibbon at Lausanne in 1848. 'We have found in this room a large old bath which belonged to Edward Gibbon.' And as imitation may be a sincere form of self-flattery, Lord John Russell wrote from Renens, near Lausanne, in 1856, 'I have got some books here, and a terrace on which I walk . . . preparing to appear as a second Gibbon.'

It was not only Gibbon's summer-house that disappeared. In 1896 his house, La Grotte, was itself pulled down to make way for a post office. Beside it, the Hôtel Gibbon already occupied part of the garden (not that where the summer-house had stood), and derived custom from the erroneous entry in Baedeker's *Guide to Switzerland*, 1905 edition, that 'in the garden behind the dining-room the historian Gibbon wrote the last part of his great work.' Now even the Hôtel Gibbon is no more, for it, in its turn, was pulled down to build offices, and there is nothing left at Lausanne to commemorate Edward Gibbon except his indestructible works and the interest which they continue to inspire.

Gibbon's bookplate

A post-mortem examination had been carried out, and a report was written by Henry Cline. From this it was clear that the upper and older part of Gibbon's tumour was an irreducible inguinal hernia, dating from his days in the Militia, containing an astonishing amount of the alimentary canal, which had drawn the stomach down from its normal position, a displacement to which the surgeons erroneously attributed his death. The wonder is that he never had an intestinal strangulation. The lower and more recent portion of the tumour was a fluid-containing bag communicating with the peritoneal cavity, and therefore not a true hydrocele, which is a closed cavity containing a yellow serous fluid, not a clear watery fluid, which collects slowly. The liver showed a large number of small tubercles, which provide the key to the problem.

The tubercles in Gibbon's liver are of interest in the history of medicine, for it was in that same year, 1793, when Gibbon was first operated on, that Matthew Baillie published his textbook of *Morbid Anatomy*, in which, for the first time, a description was given of cirrhosis of the liver, marked by numerous small tubercles, and the connection between this condition and the consumption of more alcohol than the system can tolerate. This enables Gibbon's case history to be unravelled.

Gibbon was not a 'hard drinker', but his fondness for madeira led him to consume more of it than his liver could deal with, and enough for cirrhosis to set in. As a result, the ascitic fluid in the peritoneal cavity increased faster than the liver could absorb it, whence his corpulence. Another effect of this was increased pressure on the iliac veins, which impeded the return of blood from the feet to the heart, with the result that his ankles swelled. About October 1793, the fluid in the peritoneal cavity found an outlet in a marked distension and enlargement of the already existing hernia, and gave rise to the huge fluid-containing bag, which enlarged the tumour so greatly. With the formation of this bag, the pressure inside the peritoneal cavity was reduced, the iliac veins could function normally again and the ankle swelling disappeared. This was the stage at which Gibbon called in the surgeons. Their punctures reduced the fluid-containing bag but not the hernia, which was irreducible, and as the bag communicated with the peritoneal cavity it filled again rapidly. This was one of the points on which Sir Joseph Banks particularly wanted information. The first two punctures must have been clean, but the third was septic; infection spread inwards and caused general peritonitis, fatal as usual after three days, and this was the cause of Gibbon's death.

So far, Gibbon's had been a straightforward medical history; but it becomes complicated by additional remarks contained in Francillon's letter to Levade, mentioned above. These were that the origin of all Gibbon's trouble was a venereal disease, and that it was a very long time since he had exposed himself to one. Francillon learned this from Lord Sheffield, who could have heard it only from Gibbon himself. It must have been one of the chief subjects of conversation between Sir Joseph Banks and Lord Sheffield at the dinners of the Royal Society Club.

Clinically, there is no connection between venereal disease and a hernia and fluid-containing bag, such as Gibbon suffered from. Two possible interpretations are open. Most students of Gibbon would say that he never even exposed himself to the risk of such an accident. In this case, it would be necessary to conclude that the story was suspiciously like a deliberate act of bravado on Gibbon's part, invented to compensate for his life of abstinence, to build up a picture of success with the ladies and to disarm and silence the reproaches which Lord Sheffield cannot have failed to level at his friend for having neglected his condition so long.

Alternatively, it must be supposed that Gibbon thought that he had contracted a venereal disease. Late in his life, he referred in his *Memoirs* to visiting bagnios enticed by his friends during his early years in London, and his brother-officers in the Militia may have tempted him to follow them. But on the other hand, it is reasonably clear from his journals, and from what he is known to have done, week by week, that he did not suffer from any such disease. It would therefore be necessary to conclude that Gibbon imagined he suffered from a disease that he had never contracted. This introduces a psychological problem.

The difficulty in choosing between these alternative explanations of the odd statements in Francillon's letter, lies in the fact that, in either case, Gibbon's ambivalent behaviour towards women and his aversion to marriage would be accounted for. After his juvenile passion for Suzanne Curchod, never pressed far, the number of women who flitted across his horizon was very small and left no mark. There had been a Miss Chetwynd and a Miss Fanny Page in 1761, but their intellects disappointed him and they made no impression. His fondness for Mme Bontems in Paris was filial. At Lausanne in 1763 he had a mock and ephemeral flirtation with Mme de Seigneux, but that was not serious; neither was a transient 'inclination' in Florence, nor an attempt at match-making by Mrs Holroyd in 1774. During his last period in Lausanne he showed fondness for Mme de Crousaz, Mme de Silva and Lady Elisabeth Foster, but without any semblance of result. There was also the farcical situation of Gibbon and Deyverdun agreeing that a female presence would grace their home, but neither was willing to sacrifice his bachelor status. What he showed particular affection for was 'Fanny Lausanne'.

When General Arthur Meredith Read went to Lausanne in 1879 and lived in Gibbon's house, a very old lady told him 'that the ladies of Lausanne were very proud of the historian's attentions, but she hinted that no question of passion ever entered their minds'. J.-G. Lemaistre who visited Lausanne in 1802 wrote, 'I have been assured by a person who enjoyed the confidence of that distinguished man, that the Historian of the Decline and Fall of the Roman Empire, though he frequently described in glowing colors, and perhaps in some pages with lascivious freedom, the passion of love, was a stranger to its pleasures.'

In an early attempt to appraise the sex-life of an author from his writings, Richard Porson said that Mr Gibbon's 'reflections are often just and profound, . . . nor does his humanity ever sleep unless when women are ravished.' Porson went on, 'If the History were anonymous, I should guess that these disgraceful obscenities were written by some debauchee, who having from age, or accident, or excess, survived the practice of lust, still indulged himself in the luxury of speculation; and exposed the impotent imbecility, after he had lost the vigour, of the passion.' But as the *History* was not anonymous, and Porson knew that Gibbon had written it, the attribution of the debauchery to the author was perhaps not intended to apply; and Porson made no allowance for the possibility that such bawdiness as is found in the *Decline and Fall* might be due to starvation instead of excess. J. W. Swain has suggested that, in Porson's phrase, the key word (although Porson himself might not have realized it) is 'impotent'. That was perhaps the intuitional key to the 'impertinent security' with which Jacques Necker went to bed and left Gibbon to entertain his newly married wife.

SELECT BIBLIOGRAPHY

Edward Gibbon *The History of the Decline and Fall of the Roman Empire*, Everyman edition, London: Dent, 6 vols.

Memoirs of My Life, edited by Georges A. Bonnard, London: Nelson, 1966.

Letters, edited by J. E. Norton, London: Cassell, 1956, 3 vols.

Miscellaneous Works, edited by Lord Sheffield, London: Murray, 1814 [1815], 5 vols.

'Journal de mon voyage dans quelques endroits de la Suisse', publié par Gavin de Beer et Georges A. Bonnard, *Miscellanea Gibboniana*, Lausanne: Rouge, 1952.

Journal to January 28th 1763, edited by D. M. Low, London: Chatto and Windus, 1929.

'Journal à Paris', publié par Georges A. Bonnard, *Miscellanea Gibboniana*, Lausanne: Rouge, 1952.

Journal à Lausanne, publié par Georges A. Bonnard, Lausanne: Rouge, 1945.

Journey from Geneva to Rome, edited by Georges A. Bonnard, London: Nelson, 1961.

Gavin de Beer 'Gibbon's Appreciation of Mountains', *Alpine Journal*, vol. 57, 1949.

'The Malady of Edward Gibbon', *Notes and Records of the Royal Society*, vol. 7, 1950.

Giuseppe Giarrizzo *Edward Gibbon e la cultura europea*, Napoli: Istituto, 1954.

Geoffrey Keynes *The Library of Edward Gibbon*, London: Cape, 1940.

D. M. Low *Edward Gibbon*, London: Chatto and Windus, 1937.

Arnaldo Momigliano 'Gibbon's Contribution to Historical Method', *Historia*, vol. 2, 1954, Wiesbaden.

J. E. Norton *A Bibliography of the Works of Edward Gibbon*, Oxford University Press, 1940.

Meredith Read *Historic Studies in Vaud, Berne, and Savoy*, London: Chatto and Windus, 1897.

T. J. B. Spencer *From Gibbon to Darwin*, Birmingham University, 1958.

J. W. Swain *Edward Gibbon the Historian*, London: Macmillan, 1966.

1737 27 April (O.S.) 8 May (N.S.), Gibbon born in Putney

1746 December, death of his mother

1748 January, entered Westminster School

1752 3 April, matriculated at Oxford

1753 8 June, converted Roman Catholic
30 June, arrived at Lausanne

1754 25 December, readmitted to Protestant religion

1755 21 September–20 October, toured Switzerland

1757 February, saw plays acted by Voltaire
June, met Suzanne Curchod and fell in love

1758 5 May, returned to London
24 August, wrote to Suzanne breaking off engagement

1759 12 June, commissioned as captain, South Hampshire Militia

1760 2 June, mobilized his company at Alton

1761 7 July, published *Essai sur l'étude de la littérature*

1762 23 December, Militia demobilized

1763 28 January, arrived in Paris
25 May, arrived at Lausanne

1764 18 April, left Lausanne
2 October, arrived in Rome
15 October, conceived idea of writing *Decline and Fall*

1765 25 June, returned to Buriton

1768 April, published *Mémoires littéraires de la Grande Bretagne*

1770 February, published *Critical observations on the Sixth Book of the Aeneid*
12 November, death of his father

1773 January, settled at 7 Bentinck Street
February, started writing *Decline and Fall*

1774 October, elected MP for Liskeard

1776 17 February, first volume of *Decline and Fall* published

1777 10 May, arrived in Paris
3 November, returned to London

1779 14 January, published *Vindication of fifteenth and sixteenth chapters*
3 July, appointed Commissioner of Trade and Plantations
7 October, *Mémoire Justificatif* issued by British government

1781 1 March, second and third volumes of *Decline and Fall* published
25 June, elected MP for Lymington

1783 27 September, arrived at Lausanne

1787 27 June, finished writing *Decline and Fall*
7 August, arrived in London

1788 8 May, last three volumes of *Decline and Fall* published
30 July, returned to Lausanne
December, started writing autobiographical sketches

1789 4 July, Georges Deyverdun died

1791 July–October, Lord Sheffield's family's visit to Lausanne

1793 3 April, Lady Sheffield died
3 June, Gibbon arrived in London
14 November, first puncture performed
24 November, second puncture performed

1794 13 January, third puncture performed
16 January, Gibbon died
23 January, buried in Fletching Church, Sussex

1796 31 March, *Miscellaneous Works* published by Lord Sheffield

1815 15 February, second edition of *Miscellaneous Works* published

NOTES ON THE PICTURES

(All quotations are from Gibbon unless otherwise stated)

Frontispiece. PORTRAIT OF GIBBON by Joshua Reynolds, painted in 1779 (detail). Of this splendid portrait, which cost fifty guineas, D.M.Low has said (*Edward Gibbon*, Chatto and Windus (1937), p. 1): 'We discern the full onset of learning and intellect in the great forehead and the steady, unflinching gaze; the round resolute mouth, petulant rather than sneering, is ready to mould the rolling period and the swift decisive phrases.' *By kind permission of Lord Primrose*

6 GIBBON'S FATHER, Edward Gibbon (1707–70), miniature painted by Lewis about 1757. *By courtesy of Lady Kathleen Stanley*
MAP OF PUTNEY from J.Rocque: *Ten Miles round London.* The map was drawn in 1744. The Gibbons' house stood in the north-east angle of the intersection between Upper Richmond Road (which runs more or less horizontally across the middle of the map) and Putney Park Lane (running down to between the P and T of 'Rowhampton'), and its grounds extended up to Putney Common. British Museum

7 LIME GROVE, PUTNEY, Gibbon's birthplace. From J.P.Malcolm: *Views within Twelve Miles of London* (1800)

8 THE PORTEN FAMILY by William Hogarth, *c.* 1732. From left to right: James Porten (Gibbon's grandfather), Stanier Porten (G's uncle), Catherine Porten (G's aunt), Mrs Allen (mother of Mrs James Porten and great-grandmother of G), Mrs Darell (mother of Robert Darell), Mrs James Porten (G's grandmother), Mrs Robert Darell (daughter of James Porten and aunt of G), Catherine Allen (sister of Mrs Porten), Robert Darell, Judith Porten (G's mother). *Private Collection*

9 LOVEKYN CHAPEL, Kingston Grammar School, which Gibbon attended. *By kind permission of the Headmaster*

10 WESTMINSTER SCHOOL HALL, painted by A.Pugin in 1758, Gibbon's 'cavern of fear and sorrow'. Guildhall Library. *Photo John Webb, Brompton Studio*

11 GREAT COLLEGE STREET, WESTMINSTER, 1903, drawn by Miss A.S.Illingworth. It was in this street that Gibbon's aunt, Catherine Porten, kept a boarding-house. Guildhall Library. *Photo John Webb, Brompton Studio*

12 MAGDALEN COLLEGE, OXFORD, 1730, by Vertue. The Hall, where Gibbon used to come to meals (late), is on the farther side of the quadrangle. British Museum

13 A GENTLEMAN COMMONER of the University of Oxford, in full dress, by James Roberts, 1792. This was Gibbon's academic dress. *The Curators of the Bodleian Library, Oxford*

14 THE NEW BUILDINGS of Magdalen College, Oxford, as seen from the Deer Park, by Rooker, 1787. It was in this part of the College that Gibbon had his rooms, but tradition does not indicate which they were. British Museum

15 PORTRAIT OF GIBBON as a young man, by an unknown artist. From Meredith Read: *Historic Studies* (1897)

16 RUSSELL STREET, COVENT GARDEN, London. It was in this street that John Lewis kept a bookshop where he introduced Gibbon to Father Bernard Baker. From G.W.Thornbury: *Old & New London* (1873)

17 THE INTERIOR of the Roman Catholic Chapel, in Lincoln's Inn Fields, by Pugin and Rowlandson, 1808. Guildhall Library. *Photo John Webb, Brompton Studio*

19 A FRENCH DILIGENCE. The journey across France, from Calais to Besançon, was reckoned at sixty-seven posts; in a post-chaise, the hire of which cost 144 *livres* and the post-horses and driver 351 *livres* 15 *sols*, the journey took six days. The rate of exchange was 24 *livres* to 1 guinea. From J.Carr: *The Stranger in France* (1803)

20-1 VIEW OF LAUSANNE in the eighteenth century, from the west. On the extreme left is the Château, in the Cité, near where Pavillard's house was; in the left centre is the Cathedral where Gibbon was received back into the Protestant religion; towards the right is the Eglise Saint-François behind which lies La Grotte, the house where Gibbon lived from 1784 to 1794. Engraving by I.Chauvin, *c. 1750*

22 DANIEL PAVILLARD, pasteur of Lausanne, from a portrait in oils by D.Lande, painted in 1759. *University of Lausanne*

23 PAVILLARD'S HOUSE, Rue Cité-Derrière, Lausanne, where Gibbon lodged in 1753. His room is thought to have been that on the first floor with the open window. From Sir Frederick Treves: *The Lake of Geneva* (1922)

24 ANTOINE-NOÉ DE POLIER DE BOTTENS, grand ministre de Lausanne, who catechized Gibbon, and his wife Elisabeth *née* Lagier de Pluvianes. Their daughter was Isabelle de Crousaz, afterwards Baronne de Montolieu (p. 99), Gibbon's friend. From W.de Sévery. *La vie de société dans le Pays de Vaud à la fin du dix-huitième siècle* (1911)

25 BADEN IN SWITZERLAND, where Gibbon met the Commissioners appointed to settle the Toggenburg troubles. From M.Merian: *Topographia Helvetica* (1642)

26 BERNE as seen from the east, 1758. It was there that Gibbon was received by Albrecht von Haller. British Museum

ZÜRICH, 1754, where Gibbon saw the Carolingian manuscript Bible, in which mention of the 'three Heavenly witnesses' is missing. Max A.Antonini, Zollikerberg-Zürich. *Photo Musée National Suisse, Zürich*

27 ABBEY OF OUR LADY of the Hermits at Einsideln (now spelt Einsiedeln), where Gibbon 'viewed with the contempt of a protestant . . . the Idolatrous worship' of the black image of the Virgin. From M.Merian: *op. cit.*

28 THE CHARNEL HOUSE at Morat, containing the bones of the Burgundians of Charles the Bold's army, killed in the Battle of Morat, 22 June 1476. It lay on the route of the French army which invaded Switzerland in 1798, and Mary Berry wrote in her Journal, 25 July 1803, 'the French regiment de la Côte d'Or, being unfortunately quartered at Morat in the year 1798, *nobly* destroyed it entirely, instead of, like real heroes, respecting valour in every country. Nothing remains but a few scattered bones among the weeds

which mark the place of the former enclosure.' From D.Herrliberger: *Neue und vollständige Topographie der Eydgnoszschaft* (1754)

29 ALBRECHT VON HALLER, from the portrait of C.von Stoppelaer. Haller wrote the first poem on the Alps, was the first Professor of Anatomy and Botany in George II's new University of Göttingen, was the founder of physiology as an experimental science, published the first flora of Switzerland, instituted a new method of bibliography, and was one of the greatest scholars of the eighteenth century. Gibbon's visit to him in Berne must have been an inspiration. *By permission of the Royal Society*

31 VOLTAIRE, etching of a caricature by Jean Huber. Gibbon wrote of Voltaire, then living at Lausanne, 'He received me with civility as an English youth.' From C.E.C. Russell: *Three generations of fascinating women* (1904)

32 JOHANN JACOB BREITINGER. Gibbon wrote of him: 'in our frequent letters we discussed many questions of antiquity, many passages of the Latin Classics. I proposed my interpretations and amendments: his censures, for he did not spare my boldness of conjecture, were sharp and strong; and I was encouraged by the consciousness of my strength, when I could stand in free debate against a Critic of such eminence and erudition.' From Koennecke: *Bilderatlas* (1887)

33 THE VILLAGE AND CHURCH of Crassier, the pasteur of which was Louis-Antoine Curchod, father of Suzanne, Gibbon's lady-love. From Treves, *op. cit.*

35 SUZANNE CURCHOD, afterwards Madame Jacques Necker and mother of Madame de Staël, from a portrait in oils by Duplessis. From W.de Sévery, *op. cit.*

37 THE PLACE ROYALE, now Place Stanislas, at Nancy, had been laid out between 1751 and 1757, only one year before Gibbon saw and admired it. British Museum

MAESTRICHT, *c.* 1700, where Gibbon parted from his travelling companions Jean-Louis Crousaz and Daniel Lemaire, officers in a Swiss regiment in the Dutch service (the uniform of which Gibbon wore in order to pass through France, with which Great Britain was then at war). Gibbon also called on Louis de Beaufort, author of *Dissertation sur l'incertitude des cinq premiers siècles de l'histoire romaine*. British Museum

38 THE FLOWERMARKET, Town Hall, and Groote Kerk of The Hague, by P.Fouquet, 1764. British Museum

40 BURITON HOUSE, Hampshire. Gibbon never was a countryman, and after his father's death he sold Buriton as soon as he could. *Photo copyright Country Life*

41 HIGH CHANGE in Bond Street, by Rowlandson, 1796. After his return from Lausanne, and before the embodiment of the Militia, Gibbon spent his winters in lodgings in New Bond Street, where he found himself a stranger in an unknown city, and had to make new friends for himself. Guildhall Library. *Photo John Webb, Brompton Studio*

42 JONATHAN SWIFT, by C.Jerves. *National Portrait Gallery, London*

JOSEPH ADDISON, by Godfrey Kneller. *National Portrait Gallery, London*. Both these authors, to whose works Gibbon turned his attention rather late, were his introduction to the English literary tradition. 'Wit and simplicity are their common attributes: but the style of Swift is supported by manly original vigour; that of Addison is adorned by the female graces of elegance and mildness; and the contrast of too coarse or too thin a texture is visible even in the defects of these celebrated writers.'

43 DAVID HUME, by Allan Ramsay, 1754. On the publication of the *Decline and Fall*, Hume had written to Gibbon, 'As I ran through your Volume of History with great avidity and impatience, I cannot forbear discovering somewhat of the same impatience, in returning you thanks for your agreable present, and expressing the satisfaction which the performance has given me.' *Mr Hamish Gunn, Edinburgh*

44 ALTON, HAMPSHIRE, *c.* 1835. *Curtis Museum, Alton*

45 GRENADIER CAP of the South Hampshire Militia, 1759–65. *National Army Museum, Camberley*

BLANDFORD FORUM, DORSET. 'Our stay at Blandford was very agreable, the weather fine, the quarters as good both for the officers and men as cheapness plenty and pleasantness could make them.' (Gibbon's Journal, July 1760, edited by D.M.Low, Chatto and Windus, 1929). *Dorset County Museum, Dorchester*

46 DOVER, the Town and Castle, 1762. 'At Dover, in the space of five months we began to breathe: for the men the quarters were healthy and plentiful, and our dull leisure was enlivened by the society of the fourteenth Regiment in the castle, and some sea parties in the spring.' *Dover Corporation Museum*

47 TITLE-PAGE of Gibbon's first published work, 1761. 'I was delighted by the copious extracts, the warm commendations, and the flattering predictions of the Journals of France and Holland: in England it was received with cold indifference, little read, and speedily forgotten.'

48 THE QUAI PELLETIER and Hôtel de Ville, Paris, 1760. Behind the Hôtel de Ville is the Church of Saint-Gervais. 'I devoted many hours of the morning to the circuit of Paris and the neighbourhood, to the visit of churches, and palaces, conspicuous by their architecture.' *Photo Bulloz*

THE PONT-NEUF and the Samaritaine, Paris, 1760. 'The opulence of the French capital arises from the defects of its government and Religion.' *Photo Bulloz*

49 THE SALON OF MADAME GEOFFRIN, by Lemonnier. 'Four days in the week I had a place without invitation at the hospitable tables of Mesdames Geoffrin and du Bocage, of the celebrated Helvetius and of the Baron d'Olbach: in these Symposia the pleasures of the table were improved by lively and liberal conversation; the company was select, though various and voluntary, and each unbidden guest might utter a proud and ungrateful sentence, "the brave go uninvited to the banquets of the craven".' Musée des Beaux-Arts, Rouen. *Photo Giraudon*

50 CLAUDE-ADRIEN HELVÉTIUS, whose real name was Schweizer, author of *De l'Homme*, *De l'Esprit*, and *Système de la Nature*, in all of which he combated ignorance, prejudice, superstition. Engraving by Saint-Aubin after van Loo. *Photo Giraudon*

ANNE-CLAUDE-PHILIPPE DE TUBIÈRES, comte de Caylus. 'A simple, good man who showed me the greatest kindness.' Medallion. *Photo Giraudon*

ABBÉ GUILLAUME T.F.RAYNAL, portrait by F.Bonneville, 1796

51 DENIS DIDEROT, by L.M.van Loo, 1767. Inspirer and editor of *L'Encyclopédie* and life-long opponent of religious fanaticism. Louvre, Paris. *Photo Archives Photographiques*

52 JOHN BAKER HOLROYD, afterwards Lord Sheffield, by Downman, 1780. From M.J. Stanley: *The Girlhood of Maria Josepha Holroyd, Lady Stanley of Alderley* (1896)

53 LAUSANNE, by W.MacKinnon, seen from the north. The first large building is the Château, behind which are the spires of the Cathedral. Immediately to the right of the Collège is seen the spire of the Church of Saint-François. The date of this watercolour presents a problem, for it is dated 1798, a year in which no Englishman could travel in Switzerland. *Victoria and Albert Museum, London*

55 GENEVA, by J.Rocque, 1736. Gibbon visited Geneva many times; in 1755 when he tried to sell the horse which Mr Gee had tricked him into buying, in 1757 to see some French plays acted at Carouge, in 1763 to see a performance at Voltaire's theatre at Ferney, and in 1764 on his way to Italy. British Museum

56 THE CHÂTEAU DE FERNEY, Voltaire's residence near Geneva. 'The play they acted was my favourite Orphan of China. . . . The play began at eight in the evening and ended . . . about half an hour after eleven. The whole Company was asked to stay and set down to a very elegant supper.' *Musée Voltaire, Geneva*

57 JEAN-JACQUES ROUSSEAU, by Allan Ramsay, 1766. 'I have read a little pamphlet of 38 pages [Lettre à d'Alembert sur les Spectacles] by Jean-Jacques Rousseau. It is an extract of Plato's arguments against imitative poetry and especially against the theatre. . . . The whole of the first part is so false and feeble that it astonished me. Towards the end his arguments became more specious.' *National Portrait Gallery of Scotland*

58 THE MANNER of crossing Mont Cenis, drawing by George Keate, 1755. 'I climbed Mont Cenis and descended into the plain of Piedmont, not on the back of an Elephant; but on a little osier seat in the hands of the

dextrous and intrepid chairmen of the Alps.' British Museum

59 THE BRIDGE over the Po, Turin, by Canaletto. 'The architecture and government of Turin presented the same aspect of tame and tiresome uniformity.' *Galleria Sabauda, Turin*

ISOLA BELLA, Lago Maggiore, eighteenth-century engraving. In the previous century the 'beautiful' island was Isola Madre. One of the only subjects on which Gibbon and Rousseau agreed was their appreciation of the Borromean Islands where the latter almost decided to situate his novel *La Nouvelle Héloïse*. *Photo Georgina Masson*

60 THE HARBOUR, GENOA, engraving by Jules Jarin. 'I was less amused by the marble palaces of Genoa, than by the recent memorials of her deliverance [in December 1746] from the Austrian tyranny.' From *Voyage en Italie* (1839)

FLORENCE, from the Cascine Gardens, by Thomas Patch. Gibbon spent the hot months from June to September 1764 in Florence, where he learned to acknowledge, 'at the feet of the Venus of Medicis, that the chissel may dispute the pre-eminence with the pencil, a truth in the fine arts, which cannot, on this side of the Alps be felt or understood'. *By kind permission of the Marquess of Cholmondeley*

61 SIR HORACE MANN and his friends, by Thomas Patch. 'Our envoy, Sir Horace Mann whose most serious business was that of entertaining the English at his hospitable table.' *By kind permission of Lord Talbot de Malahide*

62 THE FORUM, ROME, by Canaletto, c. 1740. In the foreground are the three remaining columns of the Temple of Castor and Pollux, behind them the Temple of Saturn, and on the Capitoline Hill the Campidoglio. 'I trod with a lofty step the ruins of the Forum; each memorable spot where Romulus stood or Tully spoke, or Caesar fell was at once present to my eye.' Royal Collection, Windsor. *By gracious permission of Her Majesty the Queen*

63 THE CAPITOLINE HILL, with (on the left) the Church of Santa Maria in Aracœli, and on the right the Campidoglio, painting by Bellotto. 'The Modern Capitol is still

grand. You ascend by a great flight of steps to a large court. The palace of the Senators is at the end. That of the Conservators, the modern Consuls on one side, and the Museum on the other.' *H.M. Treasury and the National Trust* (*Collection of Lord Egremont, Petworth*)

THE PIAZZA DEL POPOLO, ROME, by Piranesi. In the foreground, the Obelisk brought to Rome by Augustus in 10 BC. The church on the left is Santa Maria in Monte Santo, that on the right Santa Maria dei Miracoli

64 VIRGIL'S TOMB, by Giraud, 1771. According to tradition, Virgil who died on 21 September 19 BC was buried by the side of the road running from Naples to Pozzuoli, and an anonymous Roman tomb near the Roman tunnel through the cliff to Posilipo was held to be Virgil's. It has disappeared, and today, in a park at Mergellina, a small relic of a Roman tomb serves the same purpose. In his Lausanne *Journal*, Gibbon analyzed the problem of the location of Virgil's tomb, and concluded in favour of Posilipo. British Museum

65 THE PIAZZETTA, VENICE, by Canaletto. On the left, across the entrance to the Grand Canal, is the Dogana, or Customs House. Behind it is the Church of Santa Maria della Salute, erected in commemoration of deliverance from the plague of 1630. On the right is the corner of the Libreria Vecchia, built in 1536 by Jacopo Fatti Sansovino, of which Palladio (and others) considered 'that nothing more sumptuous or beautiful had been invented since the age of ancient Rome'. Gibbon's contemptuous rejection of the appeal of this building is a sad commentary on his taste for architecture. *Metropolitan Museum of Art, New York*

66 GEORGES DEYVERDUN, Gibbon's great friend who collaborated with him in producing the *Mémoires littéraires de la Grande Bretagne*, and afterwards shared his house, La Grotte, at Lausanne with him from 1784. Deyverdun's mother, Suzanne-Françoise de Teissonnière d'Ayrolles, was a cousin of Solomon Dayrolles, Lord Chesterfield's secretary, on whose advice Philip Stanhope was sent to Lausanne with

Edward Eliot, who advised Gibbon's father to send Gibbon there. From Meredith Read, *op. cit.*

JACQUES NECKER, husband of Suzanne Curchod, from a portrait in oils by Duplessis. 'The Genius of her husband has exalted him to the most conspicuous station in Europe: in every change of prosperity and disgrace he has reclined on the bosom of a faithful friend.' Their daughter Germaine became Madame de Staël. From W. de Sévery, *op. cit.*

67 TITLE-PAGE of the *Mémoires littéraires de la Grande Bretagne*, produced jointly by Gibbon and Deyverdun. 'It is not my wish to deny, how deeply I was interested in these Memoirs; of which I need not surely be ashamed; . . . I will presume to say that their merit was superior to their reputation: but it is not less true that they were productive of more reputation than emolument.'

68 PALL MALL AND ST JAMES'S PALACE, by John Bowles, 1741. 'My lodgings at Mr Taylor's Grocer's opposite to the Duke of Cumberland's Pall Mall'. The Duke lived at Schomberg House (where Gainsborough died), on the south side of Pall Mall, close to the present Royal Automobile Club. Gibbon's lodgings were therefore approximately on the site of Dent's watchmaker's shop. *By courtesy the Trustees of the British Museum*

69 GIBBON, drawing in red chalk by Thomas Patch. The attribution to Gibbon as the subject of this sketch, is based not only on the frequency with which Gibbon and Patch were guests of Sir Horace Mann at Florence in 1764, but on the following argument by Mr F.J.B. Watson: 'The cheeks later described by Miss Burney as "Brobdignatious" and of "such prodigious chubbyness that they envelop his nose so completely as to render it, in profile, absolutely invisible" were evidently already a notable feature of his countenance and have clearly struck Patch as odd. The "neat little feet" also mentioned by Miss Burney are found here too. The slightly upturned nose, the curly lips, the double chin are all in favour of the identification with Gibbon.' *Private Collection*

70 7 BENTINCK STREET, watercolour by Thomas Dibdin, 1851. Gibbon's house from 1773 to 1783 is that on the right, with the triangular-topped portico. 'My own, new clean comfortable dear house which I like better every week I pass in it. I now live which I never did before.' Guildhall Library. *Photo John Webb, Brompton Studio*

71 TITLE-PAGE of the first volume of the first edition, quarto, of *The History of the Decline and Fall of the Roman Empire* (1776). In the view of William Strahan, the Publisher, 'So able and so finished a performance, hath hardly ever before come under my inspection; and though I will not take upon me absolutely to pronounce in what manner it will be received at first by a capricious and giddy public, I will venture to say, it will ere long make a distinguished figure among the many valuable works that do honour to the present age; it will be translated into most of the modern languages, and will remain a lasting monument of the genius and ability of the author' (8 October 1775). *The Curators of the Bodleian Library, Oxford*
CORRECTED PROOF of page iv of the Preface to volume IV of *The Decline and Fall*. 'Many blemishes of style, which had been invisible in the manuscript, were discovered and corrected in the printed sheet.' *The Pierpont Morgan Library, New York*

73 GIBBON, portrait in oils by Henry Walton, *c.* 1774. This was one of a series of portraits of four friends, one of whom, Godfrey Bagnall Clarke, had been at Lausanne with Gibbon in 1763. Lord Sheffield considered it the best likeness of Gibbon. *The President and Fellows of Magdalen College, Oxford*

74 GERMAINE NECKER as a child, age about thirteen (1779), from a drawing by Carmontelle. Five years later, Gibbon wrote: 'Mademoiselle Necker one of the greatest heiresses in Europe is now about eighteen, wild, vain but goodnatured and with a much larger provision of wit than beauty.' From M.G.Parry: *Madame Necker* (1913)

75 MARIE DE VICHY-CHAMROND, marquise du Deffand, after a drawing by Carmontelle. 'Mr Walpole gave me an introduction to Madame du Deffand, an agreeable Young Lady of eighty two years of age who has constant suppers and the best Company in Paris.' Madame de Deffand was then blind, and used, when friends were introduced to her, to pass her hands over their faces. It was said that after she had done this to Gibbon, she complained that she had been the victim of a joke in bad taste. (Meredith Read, *op. cit.* 1897, vol. II, p. 391.) *Photo Giraudon*
GABRIEL BONNOT, Abbé de Mably, after Bonneville. 'I have been lately much flattered by the praise of Dr Blair and the censure of the Abbé de Mably: both of them are precisely the men from whom I could wish to obtain praise and censure. . . . The Abbé appears to hate and effects to despise every writer of his own times who has been well-received by the public.'

76 GEORGES-LOUIS LE CLERC, comte de Buffon, from the portrait by F.H.Drouais, 1761. 'The eloquent historian of Nature, who fixes our moral happiness to the mature season, in which our passions are supposed to be calmed, our duties fulfilled, our ambition satisfied, our fame and fortune established on a solid basis. . . . In private conversation, that great and amiable man added the weight of his own experience.' Private Collection. *Photo Bulloz*

77 BENJAMIN FRANKLIN, by Joseph Wright. In Paris in 1777, Gibbon '. . . dined *by accident* with Franklin'. *By permission of the Royal Society*

78 JOHN HUNTER, by Joshua Reynolds, 1786. 'The usual distractions of the Winter have been encreased by a constant daily attendance of two hours every day to Dr Hunter's Anatomy lectures which have opened to me a new and very entertaining scene within myself.' By courtesy of the President and Council of the Royal College of Surgeons of England. *Photo Courtauld Institute*

79 TITLE-PAGE of James Chelsum's *Remarks on the two last Chapters of Mr Gibbon's History*. 'The attack on me is begun, an anonymous eighteen penny pamphlet, which will get the author more Glory in the next world than in this. The Heavy troops, Watson and another are on their march.'
TITLE-PAGE of Richard Watson's *An Apology for Christianity*. 'Dr Watson now Bishop of Landaff is a prelate of a large mind and liberal spirit. I should be happy to think that his Apology for Christianity

had contributed, though at my expence to clear his Theological character.'

80 TITLE-PAGE of Gibbon's *Vindication*, '*in octavo*—for I would not print it in quarto—lest it should be bound and preserved with the History itself. My *Vindication*, expressive of less anger than contempt, amused for a moment the busy and idle metropolis; and the most rational part of the Laity, and even of the Clergy, appears to have been satisfied of my innocence and accuracy.'

81 SIR JOSHUA REYNOLDS, self-portrait, *c.* 1748. 'After viewing some portraits which he had painted in his youth, my friend Sir Joshua Reynolds acknowledged to me that he was rather humbled than flattered by the comparison with his present works.' *National Portrait Gallery, London*

OLIVER GOLDSMITH, studio of Reynolds, *c.* 1770. 'His acquaintance with Goldsmith provides one of the best stories in the Gibbon legend. Calling one morning, he found him hard at work on the *History of Greece*. "Tell me," said Goldsmith, "what was the name of that Indian king who fought Alexander?" "Montezuma," replied Gibbon promptly. "But stay," he added, as Goldsmith was innocently writing it down, "I mistake. 'Twas not Montezuma. 'Twas Porus"' (G.M.Young, *Gibbon*, 1948, p. 108). *National Portrait Gallery, London*

82 DAVID GARRICK, mezzotint after Gainsborough's painting of 1766. He retired from the stage in June 1776 and Gibbon wrote to him from Paris in the following year: 'The persons who have been in England before the fatal month of June 1776 describe with transport what they have seen and what they have felt, and those who propose to undertake the same journey express their regret that the principal object of their curiosity no longer subsists.' British Museum

83 DR SAMUEL JOHNSON, by J. Barry. George Colman: 'On the day I first sat down with Johnson, in his rusty brown, and his black worsteds, Gibbon was placed opposite to me in a suit of flower'd velvet, with a bag and sword; and Johnson's famous parallel between Dryden and Pope, might be loosely parodied, in reference to himself and Gibbon.' *National Portrait Gallery, London*

84 EDWARD ELIOT and his wife, by Richard Wilson. Mrs Eliot was Katherine Elliston, daughter of Katherine Gibbon (sister of Gibbon's father) who married Edward Elliston. Edward Elliston was the son of Hester Gibbon, sister of Gibbon's grandfather. Edward Eliot was therefore Gibbon's second cousin, his wife Gibbon's first cousin. *In the possession of Edward Eliot's descendants in Cornwall*

85 LISKEARD, the Parade and Barrell Street, 1856. 'By common consent, Liskeard, alike by general reputation and in relation to the striking personalities of many of its former members, stood well among the ancient political boroughs of Cornwall. It may not have been entirely immaculate. What small borough was in pre-reform days, or, since that epoch? But Liskeard was apparently far less contaminated by election vice than its neighbouring boroughs, and it was not without a good measure of justification that it came to be known as "the model borough".' (W.T.Lawrence: *Parliamentary Representation in Cornwall*, Truro, 1925). *Photo John Webb, Brompton Studio*

86 TITLE-PAGE of the State Paper written by Gibbon. 'As far as I can understand it has been received with some degree of approbation.' It was translated 'even into the Turkish language'. Lord Sheffield wrote, 'It obtained the highest applause in foreign courts. At Petersburg and Vienna it was currently observed by the Corps Diplomatique that the English Ministry had published a Memorial written not only with great and more usual ability, but also in French, so correct that they must have employed a Frenchman.'

87 CHARLES JAMES FOX, by Joshua Reynolds, 1784. 'I love Fox's feelings, but I detest the political principles of the man and of the party. . . . Let him do what he will I must love the dog.' *From the collection of the late Earl of Ilchester*

88 LYMINGTON QUAY, shipping cattle to the Isle of Wight, wash drawing by Rowlandson, 1784. Parliamentary representation of the borough was controlled by the Burrard family which had the right to nominate the freeman or electors. On this occasion the seat cost £3000. *Henry E. Huntington Library and Art Gallery, San Marino*

89 THE DUKE OF CUMBERLAND'S HOUSE at the end of the Steyne, Brighton, 1778. 'I have hired for three months a small pleasant house at Brighthelmstone. I flatter myself that in that admirable sea air, with the vicinity of Sheffield Place, and a proper mixture of light study in the morning and good company in the evening the summer may roll away not disagreeably. . . . I promise you not to bathe in the Sea without due preparation and advice.' *George Handelman, Hove*

90 EAST FRONT of Hampton Court Palace, engraved by Tinney. 'My friend Mr Hamilton has very obligingly lent me a ready furnished house close to the Palace, and opening by a private door into the Royal garden which is maintained for my use but not at my expence'.

91 BENJAMIN THOMPSON, afterwards Count Rumford, founder of The Royal Institution; Gibbon's fellow-passenger from Dover to Boulogne on 17 September 1783, when Gibbon was on his way to Lausanne. *Fogg Art Museum, Harvard University, Cambridge, Mass. Bequest of Edmund C. Converse*

92 LA GROTTE, Lausanne, Gibbon's house at Lausanne (under the figure 1). On the left (under the figure 2) is the house of Clavel de Brenles

93 GIBBON seated in his garden, by Michel-Vincent Brandoin, 1785-90. His sitting position, with his legs wide part, was due to his infirmity. *By courtesy the Trustees of the British Museum*

94-5 LAUSANNE, watercolour by Francis Towne, 1781. *Reproduced by permission of the Syndics of the Fitzwilliam Museum, Cambridge*

96 DR AUGUSTE TISSOT, by Angelica Kauffmann. The celebrated physician and Gibbon were firm friends, and their banter over Lady Elisabeth Foster, whom they both admired, has been preserved. Tissot: 'When your nonsense has made Lady Elisabeth seriously ill, I shall cure her.' Gibbon: 'And when Mylady has died as a result of your prescriptions, I shall make her immortal.' From W.de Sévery, *op. cit.*

97 MADAME DE STAËL, by Jean-Baptiste Isabey. 'She is a pleasant little woman.' Louvre, Paris. *Photo, Giraudon*

98 SKETCHES OF GIBBON by Lavinia, Countess Spencer, 1785. 'Lord and Lady Spencer.

I saw them almost every day at my house or their own . . . she is a charming woman. You are not ignorant of her talents, of which she has left me an agreable specimen, a drawing of the Historic muse sitting in a thoughtful posture to compose.' *By courtesy the Trustees of the British Museum*

99 ISABELLE DE MONTOLIEU, *née* Polier de Bottens. 'Has the said Mylady [Sheffield] read a novel entitled Caroline de Lichtfield, of our home manufacture; I may say of ours, since Deyverdun and myself were the judges and patrons of the Manuscript. The author who is since married a second time (Madame de Crousaz now Montolieu) is a charming woman: I was in some danger.' From W.de Sévery, *op. cit.*

100 THE PAVILION and terrace of Gibbon's house, engraved by Heath, perhaps from a drawing by Lady Elisabeth Foster. The scene of the completion of *The Decline and Fall*. From Gibbon: *Miscellaneous Works* (1814)

101 SILHOUETTES of Gibbon and Lord Sheffield, taken in 1791, and preserved by Maria Josepha Holroyd among her souvenirs of the visit to Lausanne. From M.J.Stanley, *op. cit.*

102 JOHN STREET, ADELPHI, London. Originally called The Adelphi New Tavern and Coffee-house, opened in 1777, Osborne's Hotel, where Gibbon stayed in 1787, was where Thomas Rowlandson died in 1827. From Malton: *A Picturesque Tour* (1792)

103 WEDGWOOD medallion of Gibbon, *c.* 1787. *Josiah Wedgwood and Sons, Ltd*

104 THE DE CHARRIÈRE DE SÉVERY family: 'the most perfect system of domestic happiness'. Salomon de Charrière de Sévery, formerly Grand Master of the Court of Hesse-Cassel and Controller to the Princess of Hesse-Cassel; Catherine de Charrière de Sévery, *née* de Chandieu-Villars, aunt of Benjamin Constant; their son Wilhelm de Charrière de Sévery, Gibbon's adopted son; portraits attributed to Tischbein. From W.de Sévery, *op. cit.*

105 BATH in the eighteenth century. In his last year, Gibbon stayed at York House, still a hotel, although rebuilt, near the Belvedere. From an engraving. British Museum

106 CARICATURE of Gibbon, 1788. *By courtesy the Trustees of the British Museum*

107 SHEFFIELD PLACE, SUSSEX, seat of Lord Sheffield, who bought the house from Lord De la Warr in 1769. From Gibbon: *Miscellaneous Works* (1814)

108 GIBBON with Madame de Silva, pen and ink sketch by William Wallace, 1791. Maria Josepha Holroyd wrote, 'Mr Gibbon is desperately in love with Madame de Silva, a pretty Portuguese.' *From the collection of the late Earl of Ilchester*

109 LADY SHEFFIELD, *née* Abigail Way, first wife of Gibbon's greatest friend and mother of Maria Josepha Holroyd. Portrait by Downman. Her death on 3 April 1793 was the reason for Gibbon's return to England. From M.J.Stanley, *op. cit.*

110 The CHÂTEAU BAILLIVAL at Lausanne. From an engraving after Huber. British Museum

111 GIBBON, by George Romney, 1781. It was commissioned by William Hayley who claimed that it portrayed Gibbon's social qualities better than Reynolds's portrait. *Private Collection*

112 GEORGIANA, Duchess of Devonshire, by Gainsborough, *c.* 1783. Sister of Gibbon's great friend Lord Spencer, the Duchess spent the summer of 1792 at Ouchy. *National Gallery of Art, Mellon Collection, Washington, D.C.*

113 SKETCH OF GIBBON, 1765-70. Lady Diana Beauclerk was the wife of Topham Beauclerk, Gibbon's friend and fellow-member of the Literary Club. Gibbon considered 'Lady Di one of the most accomplished women in the world.' *By courtesy the Trustees of the British Museum*

114 LADY ELISABETH FOSTER by Angelica Kauffmann, 1784 (detail). 'A bewitching animal . . . our Goddess the Eliza . . . still adorable . . . wicked . . . as seducing as ever.' *Reproduced by permission of the National Trust*

115 MADAME DE STAËL and her daughter. From M.G.Parry, *op. cit.*

116 WILLIAM BECKFORD, by John Hoppner. Gibbon's bitter enemy, who bought his library. *By courtesy of the City of Salford Museums and Art Gallery*

119 ST JAMES'S STREET, looking towards St James's Palace. No. 76, at the south-west corner of St James's Street and Little St James's Street (opposite Prunier's Restaurant), where Gibbon died, is at the bottom on the right. From Thornbury, *op. cit.*

121 MARIA JOSEPHA HOLROYD, afterwards Lady Stanley of Alderley, by Henry Edridge, 1795. From M.J.Stanley, *op. cit.*

122 FLETCHING CHURCH, Sussex. From Gibbon: *Miscellaneous Works* (1814)

123 SIR JOSEPH BANKS, by Thomas Phillips. President of the Royal Society, friend of Gibbon and Lord Sheffield. *By permission of the Royal Society*

124 DR FRÉDÉRIC SCHOLL, Gibbon's friend and physician at Lausanne, negotiated the purchase of Gibbon's library for William Beckford, who eventually presented it to him. *Bibliothèque Cantonale, Lausanne*

125 TITLE-PAGE of the catalogue of the sale of part of Gibbon's library. *Bibliothèque Cantonale, Lausanne*

126 SPECIMEN of Gibbon's handwriting. Gibbon's Journal, 1752. British Museum. *By kind permission of Sir John Murray, K.C.V.O., D.S.O.*

128 GIBBON'S BOOK-PLATE. *By courtesy the Trustees of the British Museum*

INDEX *Page numbers in italics refer to illustrations*